coolcamping

coast

D1575086

Andrew Day, Martin Dunford, David Jones,
ᴎith

The publishers assert their right to use *Cool Camping*
as a trademark of Punk Publishing Ltd.

Cool Camping: Coast

First published in the United Kingdom in 2018 by

Punk Publishing Ltd
81 Rivington Street, London EC2A 3AY
www.punkpublishing.co.uk
www.coolcamping.com
Copyright © Punk Publishing Ltd 2018

A catalogue record of this book is available from the British Library.

ISBN 978-1-906889-68-5

10 8 6 4 2 1 3 5 7 9

Contents

Introduction 5

Campsite Locator 8

Campsites at a Glance 10

South-west England 16

Beach Games 64

South & Isle of Wight 68

South-east England 90

East Anglia 94

North-east England 102

North-west England 122

Hiring a Campervan 126

North Wales 130

South Wales 152

Seaside Sites in France 178

West Scotland & Isles 184

Outer Hebrides 212

Northern Scotland 218

Glamping Alternatives 229

Index 238

Acknowledgements 240

Introduction

Britain is an island nation. Our history reflects it, our politics (now more than ever) is well and truly influenced by it and our landscapes – from craggy, Atlantic-bitten cliffs to soft subsiding sands – are defined by it.

But, for holidaymakers, to be an island nation is to be a privileged nation. In Britain, almost every single person lives within two hours of the nearest beach and even the very furthest village is still a mere 70 miles from the sea. So it's no surprise that since the very first trains hit the tracks and the very first public holidays were granted, Brits have been gorging themselves on the three Ss of the seaside: sunbathing, swimming and sandcastle-building.

For us at Cool Camping, too, the Great British coastline has been an inescapable attraction. It's now over a decade since our first guidebooks were published, picking out the best, independently run campsites in the country and offering a counterforce to behemoth resorts like Butlins and Haven Holidays. Yet while we've happily covered campsites in the peaks, wolds and downs of the inland countryside, our authors have, from the very start, been keen to do serious battle over visiting the coastal destinations. And who could blame them? With the summer sun shining down, a locally made ice-cream in one hand and an endless expanse of sand only losing itself to the blues of a perma-choppy sea, why would you want to be anywhere else?

To simply say we like the seaside, however, is to misunderstand the great diversity on offer. When it comes to choosing your patch there's still plenty of debate to be had. Cool Camping founder Jonathan Knight is an avid visitor to the South West. His eyes dreamily glaze over when he starts telling you about his trips to the Isles of Scilly (pages 16–23); the way the tiny plane to get there glides in over a dinghy-dotted bay that looks almost tropical in sunny August, and the splendid sense of other-worldliness that comes with being stuck way out in the Atlantic blue.

Author Andrew Day, meanwhile, swears by the Welsh coast. When the National Trust opened a brand-new Pembrokeshire campsite (page 168) in 2017, he was the first to jump in a campervan and report back on the surf conditions at Freshwater West beach. And, on a recent trip to Nant-y-Big (page 136), his sightings of dolphins in the bay below were only drawn into question after he also regaled us of his time in the 200-year-old Ty Coch Inn – only accessible via a walk across the beach or through a local golf course – and, in his view, "the UK's most scenic coastal pub".

Co-editor Martin Dunford cut his teeth as a travel writer getting under the skin of North Norfolk's tidal wonderlands: walking the pine forest-backed beach at Holkham Bay and riding the old wooden ferry through the marshes to Blakeney Point, where you can see a colony of grey seals (page 98). He's a particularly fond admirer of the farm-turned-campsite at Burnham Deepdale (page 100), where you can base yourself at any time of year to take in this fragmented band of coastline that's as enchanting in auburn autumnal shades as it is in busy summer.

Then, of course, there are the countless inlets and islands of North-west Scotland, soliciting solitude in any urban soul. For me, these most untouched of places hold the real appeal; campsites where you can light campfires on the beach, boil freshly picked mussels over the flames and revel in the emptiness of the landscape. Those that live there have a great sense of community, some even banding together to create community-run campsites like Cnip Grazing (page 216), and almost every campsite offers breath-taking views that only the likes of Scotland can lay claim to. Sitting in a tent at Port Bàn (page 192) and looking across the Sound of Mull to Jura, Islay and the lesser-known Isle of Gigha, you slowly begin to see how, added together, this varied UK coastline can be well over 10,000 miles in length – three times that of Spain and more than five times that of France.

There's actually no one definitive measurement for the UK's shoreline, though. Do you measure it at high tide or low? Do you include river estuaries? Is that a tiny island or just a big rock? We've had to be similarly liberal with our definition of 'coastal campsites'. Not every destination in this book lets you pitch your tent directly by the surf (see page 12 for those that do) but, with the exception of some of our glamping alternatives (pages 229–237) they're all less than a mile from the sea. Even for the very slowest of slow strollers, that's never more than 35 minutes by flip-flop flapping foot.

So where does that leave us? Well, I've dipped my toe in the water and hinted at a few of my favourite campsites on the list. But then the beauty of small, independently run locations is that every one is different. What's right for me might not hit the perfect spot for you. So take a browse through the pages, soak in the seaside suggestions and maybe take a visit to our website – coolcamping.com – where, as well as booking your holiday, you can also read other people's reviews and share your own camping story. After all, no man is an island and, on this fairest of fair isles, there are plenty of incredible campsites for every one of us.

James Warner Smith, Editor

Campsite Locator

MAP		LOCATION	PAGE
1	Troytown Farm	Isles of Scilly	16
2	Bryher Campsite	Isles of Scilly	20
3	Wild Camping Cornwall	Cornwall	24
4	Mousehole Camping	Cornwall	28
5	Teneriffe Farm	Cornwall	30
6	Elm Farm	Cornwall	32
7	Beacon Cottage Farm	Cornwall	34
8	Treveague Farm	Cornwall	38
9	East Crinnis Farm	Cornwall	40
10	Cerenety Eco Camping	Cornwall	42
11	Fairlinch Camping	Devon	46
12	Ocean Pitch	Devon	48
13	Little Meadow	Devon	52
14	Caffyns Farm	Devon	56
15	Karrageen	Devon	58
16	Beryl's Campsite	Devon	60
17	Hook Farm	Dorset	68
18	Eweleaze Farm	Dorset	70
19	Muddycreek Farm	Hampshire	74
20	Lepe Beach Campsite	Hampshire	78
21	Grange Farm	Isle of Wight	82
22	Whitecliff Bay	Isle of Wight	86
23	Shear Barn Holidays	East Sussex	90
24	Cliff House	Suffolk	94
25	Manor Farm	Norfolk	96
26	Scaldbeck Cottage	Norfolk	98
27	Deepdale Backpackers	Norfolk	100
28	Wold Farm	Yorkshire	102
29	Crows Nest	Yorkshire	104
30	Hooks House Farm	Yorkshire	106
31	Runswick Bay Camping	Yorkshire	110
32	Serenity Camping	Yorkshire	114
33	Hemscott Hill Farm	Northumberland	118
34	Walkmill Campsite	Northumberland	120
35	Ravenglass Campsite	Cumbria	122
36	Trwyn Yr Wylfa	Conwy	130
37	Aberafon	Gwynedd	132
38	Mynydd Mawr	Gwynedd	134
39	Nant-y-Bîg	Gwynedd	136
40	Graig Wen	Gwynedd	140
41	Cae Du Farm	Gwynedd	144
42	Smugglers Cove Boatyard	Gwynedd	148
43	Hill Fort Tipis	Pembrokeshire	152
44	Celtic Camping	Pembrokeshire	154
45	Dunes at Whitesands	Pembrokeshire	156
46	Porthclais Farm	Pembrokeshire	158
47	Shortlands Farm	Pembrokeshire	162
48	Walton West Campsite	Pembrokeshire	164
49	Gupton Farm	Pembrokeshire	168
50	Hillend	Gower	172
51	Skysea Campsite	Gower	174
52	Heritage Coast Campsite	Glamorgan	176
53	Lochranza	Isle of Arran	184
54	Muasdale	Argyll	188
55	Port Bàn	Argyll	192
56	Ardnamurchan	Argyll	194
57	Cleadale Campsite	Isle of Eigg	198
58	Invercaimbe	Inverness-shire	200
59	Camus More	Isle of Skye	202
60	Sands	Wester Ross	206
61	Badrallach	Ross-shire	210
62	Lickisto Blackhouse	Isle of Harris	212
63	Cnip Grazing	Isle of Lewis	216
64	Scourie	Sutherland	218
65	Sango Sands	Sutherland	222
66	Dunnet Bay	Caithness	226
67	Cotna Eco Retreat	Cornwall	229
68	Free Range Escapes	Cornwall	229
69	Coastal Cabins	Devon	229
70	Owl Valley	Devon	229
71	Knaveswell Farm	Dorset	230
72	Vintage Vacations	Isle of Wight	230
73	Elmley Nature Reserve	Kent	230
74	The Shepherd's Hide	Essex	230
75	The Grove	Norfolk	233
76	Amber's Bell Tents	Norfolk	233
77	Little Otchan Hut	Yorkshire	233
78	Woodman's Huts	Cumbria	233
79	Mountain Lodge	Conwy	234
80	Bach Wen Farm	Gwynedd	234
81	Llwyndu Farm Hut	Gwynedd	234
82	Stackpole Under the Stars	Pembrokeshire	234
83	Frankshore Cabins	Pembrokeshire	237
84	Runach Arainn	Isle of Arran	237
85	Harvest Moon	East Lothian	237
86	Sheiling Holidays	Isle of Mull	237

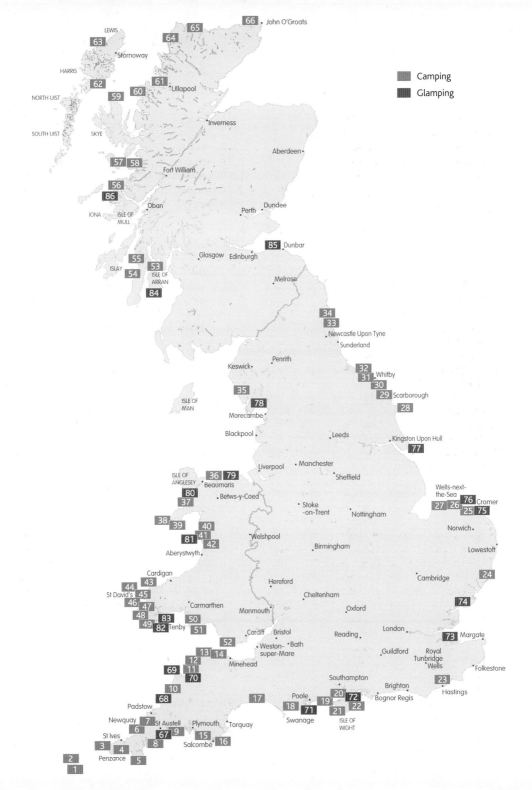

Camping

Glamping

Campsites at a Glance

COOL FOR CAMPFIRES

1	Troytown Farm	16
3	Wild Camping Cornwall	24
6	Elm Farm	32
10	Cerenety Eco Camping	42
11	Fairlinch Camping	46
14	Caffyns Farm	56
16	Beryl's Campsite	60
18	Eweleaze Farm	70
19	Muddycreek Farm	74
20	Lepe Beach Campsite	78
26	Scaldbeck Cottage	98
27	Deepdale Backpackers	100
28	Wold Farm	102
33	Hemscott Hill Farm	118
34	Walkmill Campsite	120
37	Aberafon (beach only)	132
38	Mynydd Mawr	134
40	Graig Wen	140
41	Cae Du Farm	144
42	Smugglers Cove Boatyard	148
43	Hill Fort Tipis	152
44	Celtic Camping	154
45	Dunes at Whitesands	156
47	Shortlands Farm	162
48	Walton West Campsite	164
50	Hillend	172
52	Heritage Coast Campsite	176
55	Port Bàn (beach only)	192
58	Invercaimbe	200
59	Camus More	202
60	Sands (beach only)	206
61	Badrallach	210
62	Lickisto Blackhouse	212
63	Cnip Grazing	216

COOL FOR CAMPERVANS

4	Mousehole Camping	28
5	Teneriffe Farm	30
6	Elm Farm	32
7	Beacon Cottage Farm	34

8	Treveague Farm	38
9	East Crinnis Farm	40
10	Cerenety Eco Camping	42
11	Fairlinch Camping	46
12	Ocean Pitch	48
13	Little Meadow	52
14	Caffyns Farm	56
15	Karrageen	58
16	Beryl's Campsite	60
17	Hook Farm	68
18	Eweleaze Farm	70
21	Grange Farm	82
22	Whitecliff Bay	86
23	Shear Barn Holidays	90
24	Cliff House	94
25	Manor Farm	96
27	Deepdale Backpackers	100
28	Wold Farm	102
29	Crows Nest	104
30	Hooks House Farm	106
31	Runswick Bay Camping	110
32	Serenity Camping	114
34	Walkmill Campsite	120
35	Ravenglass Campsite	122
36	Trwyn Yr Wylfa	130
37	Aberafon	132
38	Mynydd Mawr	134
39	Nant-y-Big	136
40	Graig Wen	140
41	Cae Du Farm	144
43	Hill Fort Tipis	152
44	Celtic Camping	154
46	Porthclais Farm	158
47	Shortlands Farm	162
48	Walton West Campsite	164
49	Gupton Farm	168
50	Hillend	172
51	Skysea Campsite	174
53	Lochranza	184
54	Muasdale	188
55	Port Bàn	192

56	Ardnamurchan	194
58	Invercaimbe	200
59	Camus More	202
60	Sands	206
61	Badrallach	210
62	Lickisto Blackhouse	212
63	Cnip Grazing	216
64	Scourie	218
65	Sango Sands	222
66	Dunnet Bay	226

DOG FRIENDLY (on leads mostly)

1	Troytown Farm	16
4	Mousehole Camping	28
5	Teneriffe Farm	30
6	Elm Farm	32
7	Beacon Cottage Farm	34
8	Treveague Farm	38
9	East Crinnis Farm	40
10	Cerenety Eco Camping	42
11	Fairlinch Camping	46
13	Little Meadow	52
14	Caffyns Farm	56
15	Karrageen	58
16	Beryl's Campsite	60
17	Hook Farm	68
18	Eweleaze Farm	70
19	Muddycreek Farm	74
21	Grange Farm	82
22	Whitecliff Bay	86
23	Shear Barn Holidays	90
24	Cliff House	94
25	Manor Farm	96
26	Scaldbeck Cottage	98
27	Deepdale Backpackers	100
29	Crows Nest	104
30	Hooks House Farm	106
31	Runswick Bay Camping	110
32	Serenity Camping	114
34	Walkmill Campsite	120
35	Ravenglass Campsite	122

36	Trwyn Yr Wylfa	130
37	Aberafon	132
38	Mynydd Mawr	134
39	Nant-y-Big	136
40	Graig Wen	140
41	Cae Du Farm	144
42	Smugglers Cove Boatyard	148
43	Hill Fort Tipis	152
44	Celtic Camping	154
46	Porthclais Farm	158
47	Shortlands Farm	162
48	Walton West Campsite	164
49	Gupton Farm	168
51	Skysea Campsite	174
52	Heritage Coast Campsite	176
53	Lochranza	184
54	Muasdale	188
55	Port Bàn	192
56	Ardnamurchan	194
58	Invercaimbe	200
59	Camus More	202
60	Sands	206
61	Badrallach	210
62	Lickisto Blackhouse	212
63	Cnip Grazing	216
64	Scourie	218
65	Sango Sands	222
66	Dunnet Bay	226

OPEN ALL YEAR

22	Whitecliff Bay	86
24	Cliff House	94
27	Deepdale Backpackers	100
31	Runswick Bay Camping	110
35	Ravenglass Campsite (almost)	122
40	Graig Wen	140
44	Celtic Camping	154
47	Shortlands Farm	162
51	Skysea Campsite	174
61	Badrallach	210

GOOD DISABLED ACCESS

4	Mousehole Camping	28
8	Treveague Farm	38
9	East Crinnis Farm	40
13	Little Meadow	52
14	Caffyns Farm	56
15	Karrageen	58
22	Whitecliff Bay	86
23	Shear Barn Holidays	90
24	Cliff House	94
27	Deepdale Backpackers	100
29	Crows Nest	104
31	Runswick Bay Camping	110
32	Serenity Camping	114
35	Ravenglass Campsite	122

38	Mynydd Mawr	134
44	Celtic Camping	154
49	Gupton Farm	168
51	Skysea Campsite	174
52	Heritage Coast Campsite	176
53	Lochranza	184
60	Sands	206
61	Badrallach	210
66	Dunnet Bay	226

PLAYIN' AROUND
(campsites with playgrounds)

5	Teneriffe Farm	30
7	Beacon Cottage Farm	34
8	Treveague Farm	38
9	East Crinnis Farm	40
17	Hook Farm	68
20	Lepe Beach Campsite	78
21	Grange Farm	82
22	Whitecliff Bay	86
23	Shear Barn Holidays	90
24	Cliff House	94
25	Manor Farm	96
29	Crows Nest	104
37	Aberafon	132
50	Hillend	172
55	Port Bàn	192
60	Sands	206

PADDLIN' AROUND

(campsites with swimming pools)

22	Whitecliff Bay	86
23	Shear Barn Holidays	90
29	Crows Nest	104

HORSIN' AROUND

(campsites with farm animals)

5	Teneriffe Farm	30
8	Treveague Farm	38
10	Cerenety Eco Camping	42
14	Caffyns Farm	56
19	Muddycreek Farm	74
21	Grange Farm	82
25	Manor Farm	96
33	Hemscott Hill Farm	118
34	Walkmill Campsite	120
44	Celtic Camping	154

RIGHT BESIDE THE SEA

1	Troytown Farm	16
2	Bryher Campsite	20
12	Ocean Pitch	48

18	Eweleaze Farm	70
19	Muddycreek Farm	74
20	Lepe Beach Campsite	78
21	Grange Farm	82
24	Cliff House	94
26	Scaldbeck Cottage	98
28	Wold Farm	102
29	Crows Nest	104
33	Hemscott Hill Farm	118
37	Aberafon	132
39	Nant-y-Big	136
40	Graig Wen	140
41	Cae Du Farm	144
42	Smugglers Cove Boatyard	148
44	Celtic Camping	154
46	Porthclais Farm	158
50	Hillend	172
51	Skysea Campsite	174
54	Muasdale	188
55	Port Bàn	192
56	Ardnamurchan	194
58	Invercaimbe	200
59	Camus More	202
60	Sands	206

61	Badrallach	210
62	Lickisto Blackhouse	212
63	Cnip Grazing	216
64	Scourie	218
65	Sango Sands	222
66	Dunnet Bay	226

RIGHT BESIDE A RIVER

21	Grange Farm	82
34	Walkmill Campsite	120
37	Aberafon	132
40	Graig Wen	140
42	Smugglers Cove Boatyard	148
53	Lochranza	184
58	Invercaimbe	200
60	Sands	206

NEAR THE MOUNTAINS

35	Ravenglass Campsite	122
36	Trwyn Yr Wylfa	130
37	Aberafon	132
40	Graig Wen	140
41	Cae Du Farm	144

42	Smugglers Cove Boatyard	148
53	Lochranza	184
56	Ardnamurchan	194
57	Cleadale Campsite	198
58	Invercaimbe	200
59	Camus More	202
60	Sands	206
61	Badrallach	210
62	Lickisto Blackhouse	212
63	Cnip Grazing	216
64	Scourie	218
65	Sango Sands	222

SHORT WALK TO THE PUB

1	Troytown Farm	16
2	Bryher Campsite	20
4	Mousehole Camping	28

6	Elm Farm	32
8	Treveague Farm	38
9	East Crinnis Farm	40
10	Cerenety Eco Camping	42
12	Ocean Pitch	48
17	Hook Farm	68
19	Muddycreek Farm	74
21	Grange Farm	82
23	Shear Barn Holidays	90
24	Cliff House	94
26	Scaldbeck Cottage	98
27	Deepdale Backpackers	100
29	Crows Nest	104
31	Runswick Bay Camping	110
32	Serenity Camping	114
33	Hemscott Hill Farm	118
35	Ravenglass Campsite	122

36	Trwyn Yr Wylfa	130
38	Mynydd Mawr	134
40	Graig Wen	140
47	Shortlands Farm	162
50	Hillend	172
52	Heritage Coast Campsite	176
53	Lochranza	184
65	Sango Sands	222

WOODLAND CAMPING PITCHES

17	Hook Farm	68
24	Cliff House	94
35	Ravenglass Campsite	122
40	Graig Wen	140
42	Smugglers Cove Boatyard	148

Find and book your perfect camping holiday

To instantly check availability for hundreds of camping and glamping sites and book at the best price, visit

coolcamping.com

Troytown Farm

St Agnes, Isles of Scilly TR22 0PL   01720 422360   troytown.co.uk

If camping on the tiny island of St Agnes isn't exciting enough, it's certainly an adventure getting there. Take your pick from a boat or plane for the journey to one of the Isles of Scilly's two main islands, St Mary's. The plane has the edge for maximum thrill, a tiny eight-seater bouncing about on the winds. Bag one of the front seats, inches from the whirring propellers, for a bird's-eye view of the 100-odd islands that make up the archipelago. Then it's on to a catamaran for the trip to St Agnes, and the turquoise waters of Porth Conger, and finally, a tractor ride – for your luggage at least. Most people choose to let their bags go ahead and walk the 20 minutes to the campsite, a scenic stroll that provides a stunning introduction to the island.

At just one mile in diameter, St Agnes is one of the smallest of the inhabited Scilly islands. It's a beautiful, rugged place that has seen little change since Celtic times, a forgotten outpost of England's western extremities. The majority of the island's 70 inhabitants work in flower farming during the winter months, as they have done for generations, although tourism is now just as important to the economy. Even so, there are only a handful of B&Bs on the island, and most people who come here stay at Troytown Farm, England's westernmost campsite.

Its position couldn't be any more remote or any more spectacular, clinging to the western foreshore of the island, just feet away from the rock-calmed Atlantic waters that look as if they might engulf the campsite at high tide. To one side, the beautiful curve of sand of Periglis Beach extends into the sea. To the other, bold, intriguing rock formations add interest to the heather-covered coastal landscape. It's a magical wilderness that feels like the ends of the earth – and, in fact, it almost is; the nearest neighbours to the south-west are New Yorkers.

There are small, separate fieldlets with low hedges and walls offering protection from the elements, but this can be a windy island so come prepared. When the sun shines, though, this place is perfect. You can play in rock pools, spot rare, migrating birds or just sling up a hammock and listen to the waves gently lapping the foreshore. At night the lack of light pollution affords incredible views of the Milky Way, too.

St Agnes may be remote, but it's fairly self-sufficient. Troytown Farm has a small dairy herd producing milk and cream for the island. They also rear pigs and grow vegetables, so most survival essentials are available at the onsite shop. The rest of life's necessities are available by the pint at The Turks Head in Porth Conger, the island's only pub. Perched on the hillside overlooking the bay and the adjacent islet of The Gugh, it might just win the prize for best beer garden view in England.

St Agnes is also blessed with some fantastic beaches. As well as Periglis Beach there are small, sheltered sands at Cove Vean on the east shore and a sandbar at Porth Conger, where you can splash about in the waves or walk across to The Gugh at low tide. But for great sunset views, head back to Periglis – and see if you can spot the Statue of Liberty in the distance.

COOL FACTOR One of England's most naturally beautiful campsites, offering extreme Atlantic isolation.

WHO'S IN Tents, glampers, dogs and well-behaved groups – yes. Motorhomes, caravans – no.

ON SITE Around 40 grass pitches, plus 5 bell tents available for hire (furnished with mattresses, cooking and food storage facilities and more). A traditional granite building houses toilets, showers (tokens needed), coin-operated washing machines and dryers, shaver points and babychanging facilities. There's also an onsite shop and buckets, spades and crabbing lines are provided to keep the kids (or young at heart) busy.

OFF SITE Island Wildlife Tours (01720 422212) run great tours of the islands, or you could try snorkelling with seals with Scilly Diving (01720 422848).

FOOD & DRINK The farm shop on site sells its own dairy products, veg and some meat. For great seafood try the High Tide Seafood Restaurant (01720 423869), a short walk from the site, while The Turk's Head (01720 422434) in Porth Conger serves food and beer that are surpassed only by the incredible views.

GETTING THERE The Isles of Scilly lie 28 miles off the coast of Cornwall and are reached by plane or ferry from the mainland – contact Isles of Scilly Travel (islesofscilly-travel.co.uk; 01736 334220) for further information. From St Mary's, a smaller boat brings you to St Agnes in around 15 minutes. When you arrive on St Agnes, you will be met at the quay to transport your luggage to the site (and back when you leave). The campsite is an easy 15-minute walk from there.

PUBLIC TRANSPORT Ferries to Scilly depart from Penzance where the train station is close to the ferry port and well connected to London. Flights to Scilly operate from Exeter, Newquay and Land's End airports.

OPEN March–October; winter by arrangement.

THE DAMAGE Adults (or children 5yrs and over) £10, young children (1–4yrs) £5.50, babies free. Bell tent stays from £51 per night or £335 a week. Luggage transportation from the quay to the campsite £3 per person.

Bryher Campsite

Jenford, Bryher, Isles of Scilly TR23 0PR   01720 422068   bryhercampsite.co.uk

The tiny island of Bryher, Isles of Scilly, has two distinct faces. To the south and east, calm waters fill the narrow, sheltered channel between the island and its larger cousin, Tresco. Boats come and go while sunbathers enjoy the sandy beaches at Green Bay and the secluded cove of Rushy Bay. The north-western shores, however, are a jagged jumble of weather-torn rocks, beaten by relentless Atlantic waves. Gales sometimes lash this coast with thousand-ton breakers, and spots like Badplace Hill and Hell Bay have earned their names for a reason.

It's these characteristics that make Bryher special. The sandy bays to the south are backed by dunes and provide ample opportunity for sunbathing, swimming and snorkelling, although the water can be a little nippy. Just beyond, Samson Hill is the southernmost point, with far-reaching views across the Scillies, while the exposed, heather-covered plateau at the north end of the island is dotted with prehistoric burial cairns.

A short climb uphill from the boat jetty, where a tractor collects your bags, is Bryher campsite. Despite boasting views of the harbour, Tresco Channel and Cromwell's Castle to the east and the open Atlantic to the west, it still occupies a wonderfully sheltered spot between two higher hills. It's a discreet, tents-only site, which blends effortlessly into the landscape of the island, although the recent addition of luxury bell tents means you can turn up with little more than a toothbrush and sleeping bag if that's what you're after. It's undoubtedly a beautiful place – best appreciated in spring or summer when warm, sunny days turn all of Bryher into an island paradise.

COOL FACTOR A peaceful, sheltered camping paradise on tiny Bryher island.

WHO'S IN Tents, glampers and well-behaved groups – yes. Dogs, motorhomes and caravans – no.

ON SITE 5 camping fields with 78 pitches and 2 pre-pitched bell tents, plus a separate games field, football goals and a volleyball net. Toilets, basins and token-operated showers; coin-operated hairdryers and a shaver point. Washing machine, tumble dryer and a freezer for ice packs. Bell tents are fully equipped (including dining and cooking gear), just bring towels and bedding. Mobile phone-charging available. Tractor service for luggage from the quay (bookable in advance). The site stocks camping gas and other fuel, though for larger, non-disposable gas you must provide your own container.

OFF SITE Bennett Boatyard (07979 393206) offers small motor boats, sailing dinghies, kayaks and stand-up paddle boards. Or jump on one of the regular the inter-Island ferry connections to the larger islands of St Mary's and Tresco. If it rains, check out local artworks at the Golden Eagle Studio (01720 422671), near to the Hell Bay Hotel where, incidentally, spa treatments are another rainy day option.

FOOD & DRINK The cosy Fraggle Rock (01720 422222), the Scillies' smallest pub, is just a few minutes' walk down the hill towards the quay. The contemporary Hell Bay Hotel (01720 422947) has an outside bar overlooking the sea and serves outstanding local seafood both in its restaurant and the more casual Crab Shack. Bryher Shop offers an excellent selection of food and drink, as well as freshly baked bread and pastries. You can also pre-order shopping or delivery to the campsite on arrival.

GETTING THERE See p.19 for access to the Isles of Scilly. From St Mary's, hop on a smaller inter-island ferry to reach Bryher. When you check in your luggage at Penzance Quay or the airport it will be taken all the way to the campsite for you. The campsite is a 5–10 minute walk from the quay.

OPEN Late March–October.

THE DAMAGE Camping £10.75 per person; under-4s camp free. Bell tents from £51 per night or £340 per week.

Wild Camping Cornwall

Penwith Heritage Coast, St Just, Penzance, Cornwall TR19 7TS   07842 888645   wildcampingcornwall.co.uk

If good things come in small packages, then it's no wonder that truly amazing things are to be found at this teeny-tiny campsite on Cornwall's Penwith Heritage Coast. Home to just two wild camping pitches, a bell tent and an enchanting gypsy caravan, this pocket-sized hideout between the moors and the beaches is one for those looking to get off-grid and back to nature; a place where campfires, coastal walks and late-night stargazing are all routine.

In fact, despite its size, the campsite feels positively spacious. Every pitch has its own independent area – a whopping 50m by 50m, basically a field for each camper – while an adjacent 12-acre woodland, dimpled by small ponds, gives the place a far wider reach; you can follow trails into the trees and explore the protected wildlife habitats straight from your tent. The facilities are modest and suit the campsite's name, with composting toilets, gas-powered showers and no electricity, though a covered dining area and simple cooking facilities are a welcome treat. Glampers, of course, also have the added luxury of proper beds and furnishings, all ready and waiting their arrival.

The size of the campsite also lends it a wonderfully personable feel. Owner Francesca greets you in the car park and provides you with a welcome pack of logs for the campfire as she shows you to your pitch. She can also help organise activities, working with local company Future Tracks, who provide onsite courses covering everything from bushcraft to archery.

It's when you venture beyond the gate, though, that the real beauty of this campsite is revealed. Clamber back inland and across to Watch Croft, the highest point in West Penwith, for dazzling views out to sea and the ruins of the local, clifftop mines (as seen in the BBC's *Poldark*) or walk the 20-minute valley trail down to the coast. Portheras Cove offers the nearest beach, a stretch of sand between great rocky jaws, while St Ives Bay and St Ives itself are within easy driving distance.

COOL FACTOR Off-grid and wild with just a handful of pitches.

WHO'S IN Glampers, tent campers – yes. Campervans, caravans, dogs, large groups – no.

ON SITE 2 huge tent pitches, 1 bell tent and 1 gypsy caravan. 3 compost toilets, 2 gas-powered showers, a covered dining area and washing-up sinks. Each pitch, bell tent and gypsy caravan has a firepit. Bell tents also feature a double bed (bedding and linen provided), soft furnishings and a wood-burning stove. The gypsy caravan has a built-in double bed and a kitchen area with all necessary equipment. Outdoor education company Future Tracks runs weekly bushcraft and traditional archery sessions as well as other activities.

OFF SITE It's a ½-mile walk to sandy Portheras Cove, where the footpath links up with the South West Coast Path. Boat Cove, a little further west, is tucked in a tiny inlet between Pendeen Lighthouse and Portheras Cove and makes for a pleasant diversion. Directly behind the campsite, enjoy great views from the raised moorland where Chun Quoit, Men-An-Tol and several stone circles can be discovered.

FOOD & DRINK Stroll 500m to the café at Morvah School-house Art Gallery (01736 787808) or hop in the car to the nearest pubs – it's 3 miles to Zennor, home to the excellent Gurnards Head (01736 796928) and Tinners Arms (01736 796927). It's around the same distance, in the opposite direction, to St Just – the best place to go for groceries.

GETTING THERE From Penzance take the A3071 to St Just and ¾ mile after passing through Newbridge turn right on to the B3318 to Pendeen, where you turn right onto the B3306, signposted to St Ives. After ¾ mile, on a sharp blind bend, take the farm track on your right. Follow this for 300m past Higher Kiegwin Farm until you see the 'Wild Camping' sign directing you into the field on your left.

PUBLIC TRANSPORT St Ives has the closest train station, from where buses run to nearby Morvah (or it's a 10-minute walk) – get the First Kernow A3 or the number 7.

OPEN Late June–early September.

THE DAMAGE Tent pitch and up to 4 people from £38 per night. Glamping from around £60 per night.

Mousehole Camping

Trungle Parc, Paul, Mousehole, Penzance, Cornwall TR19 6AZ   07901 752088   mouseholecamping.co.uk

We've heard of campsites with a football pitch on offer, but how about the other way round? Tucked in the far south-western corner of the British Isles, Mousehole Camping in Cornwall offers exactly that – a minor league football club that have introduced a handy little campsite adjacent to their pitch.

Trungle Parc is home to the South West Peninsula League's finest, Mousehole AFC. Their idea is nothing short of genius. The essential facilities have long been in place – showers, toilets and sinks inside the main changing rooms and a clubhouse bar, with cheap drinks and a fantastic community atmosphere – while the field is purposefully flat and well drained, the ideal conditions for camping. If you don't mind that slightly makeshift, pop-up campsite feel than you can't go far wrong. Tents are welcome in July and August (when the footy season is over) but if you've come by campervan and secured one of five prized pitches that are open February–September, there's a free game to watch every Saturday!

Of course, the real success of this campsite doesn't stem from the fact that the facilities are well maintained and prices kept conveniently low (though that certainly helps), but more importantly from its knock-your-socks-off location which, at the end of the day, is the real reason they can get away with opening up a corner of the ground and just leaving you to it!

A stroll away from the campsite entrance, the tiny village of Paul is an endearing little place, with a local pub – the Kings Arms – that's a cosy, old stone haunt with a couple of picnic benches outside, looking across to the parish church opposite. The centre of the village's history, this towered old building is said to have been founded in the year 409 by the Welsh saint, Paul Aurelian. Today's structure actually dates from the year 1600, after the invitingly isolated Penwith Peninsula was sacked and burned by marauding Spaniards five years earlier.

The campsite – or, more accurately, the football club – takes its name from the next village over, a tiny cluster of houses encircling a beautiful old harbour. It was here that the Spanish first landed, with a plaque outside the only surviving building that reads 'Squire Jenkyn Keigwin was killed here 23 July 1595 defending this house against the Spaniards'. Today the picture-perfect spot, speckled with colourful dinghies, boasts a sandy crescent beach when the tide is out and excellent crabbing opportunities from the far harbour walls – the first discovery of many along this stretch of heritage coastline. This is a peninsula on the very edge of the country with all the drama, history and intrigue that you could ask for.

COOL FACTOR A basic but spectacularly located campsite, resourcefully based around the local football club's facilities.

WHO'S IN Tents, campervans, families, groups, dogs – yes. Caravans and large motorhomes – no.

ON SITE Around 25 grass pitches, plus 5 harder spots for campervans. The campsite uses the football club's changing-room facilities, including toilets, solar-powered showers and washbasins. The clubhouse (open during busy times) sells soft and alcoholic drinks and has a pool table, table football, TV and ample parking. There is a large stainless steel sink for washing-up and the referee's room has a freezer for ice packs. Campfires are not permitted, unfortunately, and BBQs must be raised off the grass.

OFF SITE Walk the 15 minutes to picture-perfect Mousehole, an attractive fishing village centred around its old harbour. Wander the cobbled streets visiting the art galleries and independent shops or catch a bus from there to Penzance, which is just 3 miles from the campsite. St Michael's Mount (01736 710265) is then just a 20-minute walk along the seafront and across the beach – you can walk the causeway at low tide or take the boat when it's high.

FOOD & DRINK At busy times the MFC clubhouse opens, serving well-priced drinks. Just 500m away, Paul has a great village local, The Kings Arms (01736 731224), serving hearty pub meals and a wide range of beers; it also has Wi-Fi. It's around a 15-minute downhill walk to the village of Mousehole where there are more options, including the brilliant Old Coastguard (01736 731222). Penzance is also less than 10 minutes' drive away and has supermarkets, pubs and a great range of takeaways and restaurants.

GETTING THERE From Penzance, head towards Newlyn. At the crossroads go straight across and up the hill. Continue to the top of the hill for 1 mile until you reach a T-junction (signposted Mousehole). Turn left and, in half a mile, before Paul's church, turn right. The campsite entrance is at the end of the road, next to Paul Cricket Club.

OPEN Tents July–August; campervans February–September.

THE DAMAGE Pitch and 2 people from £18. Extra people £2. Under-2s free.

Teneriffe Farm

Predannack, Mullion, Helston, Cornwall TR12 7EZ 01326 240293 nationaltrust.org.uk

Don't expect the wow-factor to hit you as soon as you arrive at Teneriffe Farm. On first impressions it's just a very pleasant place to pitch up, hemmed in by farmland, and with a blaze of Atlantic blue peeking above the hedges. Beyond this there are no obvious frills, save for the swings and slide of the children's play area. But that's just the point: camping should be a simple pursuit and it's always best if your focus is on nature, starry nights and the Great Outdoors. And Teneriffe Farm is a perfect place for all three.

Close to the Lizard National Nature Reserve, 10 minutes on foot from the South West Coast Path and a 40-minute stroll from the pretty harbour of Mullion Cove, the location is a gem. The acquisition of this cliff-fringed site by the National Trust a few years ago was part of a project to breathe new life into the landscape by re-joining the neighbouring land and running a viable farm where there hadn't been one for years. The result, today, is that tenant farmer Will Watson and his family commendably manage a herd of hardy Dexter and Red Devon cattle alongside the campsite – the herds' wind-blown, browny-red figures grazing on the cliffs and fields beyond the camping meadows.

Along with its exceptional location, Teneriffe is widely recognised as one of the National Trust's most important farms for nature conservation. Rare plants – rushes, ferns, liverworts and wild asparagus – thrive on the cliffs' thin soils, while Will annually sows plots of bird seed, which act like living bird tables, attracting flocks of skylarks in their droves. No surpise, then, that the campsite has the same magnetic effect on nature-lovers.

COOL FACTOR Nature-friendly camping on the farm.

WHO'S IN Tents, campervans, caravans, dogs (maximum 2 per pitch) – yes. Groups – no.

ON SITE 24 generous pitches (14 hook-ups) and an overflow field, plus a handful of camping pods. The ablutions block was renovated in 2018 and includes toilets, powerful showers, a laundry and an undercover washing-up area. Ice-pack freezing and phone-charging facilities. Children's play area. Pods are simply furnished, with 4 mattresses, a small heater, lights and a plug socket. Bikes can be hired and delivered to the campsite from a local provider (ask at reception). Free weekly farm walks with Will in the school summer holidays. Free-range hens roam around the campsite.

OFF SITE Mullion Cove is a short drive or 40-minute walk from here, and you can go on a kayaking trip with Lizard Adventure (07845 204040) or walk over the cliffs to Poldhu via the Marconi Centre, where the first transatlantic message was sent in 1901. Turn the walk into a 4-mile loop via Mullion village.

FOOD & DRINK For the best fish and chips in the area it's worth the 10-minute drive to The Smugglers in Lizard village (01326 290763).

GETTING THERE From the A3083 (Helston–Lizard) head right on the B2296 through Mullion. Before Mullion Cove, turn left to Predannack and follow the road for 1 mile until you see the campsite.

PUBLIC TRANSPORT The bus between Helston and Lizard stops at Mullion, just over a mile away. From there it's a pleasant walk along the coastal path.

OPEN Easter–November.

THE DAMAGE A pitch and 2 people £10–£19 per night. Adults £4, children (5–15yrs) free–£2, under-4s free. Dogs £1. Electric hook-up £4. Pods from £30 per night.

Elm Farm

Nancekuke, Redruth, Cornwall TR16 5UF   01209 891498   elmfarm.biz

Capitalising on its prime location beside the Mineral Tramways cycle network, Elm Farm is a campsite-cum-cycle centre with a cute little café thrown in for good measure. It's a family-run establishment less than two miles by bike from the nearest beach – pick from Portreath and Porthtowan or explore secret swimming holes like Fisherman's Cove – while, inland, trails weave you through the county's 19th-century mining history, past moonscape quarries and ancient copper and tin mines.

The site's two camping meadows are simple, off-grid affairs and have been left purposefully alone in order to maintain their natural appeal – to people and wildlife alike. Buzzards are common, barn owls are sometimes heard in the night and stoats have even been spotted, hidden beyond the great elm trees that border the field and give the farm its name. With just 25 pitches there's ample space for ball games, and the pair of family shower rooms and compost toilets are more than adequate, though the café has flushing loos if you prefer.

If you haven't brought your own bikes, you can hire them from the café and cycle shop. Even as you stroll to collect them, your eyes are drawn to the view beyond. Laity Moor stretches in the distance to Carn Brea Hill, one of the highest points in the area from which you can see both the north and south Cornwall coast. If you don't fancy schlepping up there, you can stick to the easy ride down to the beach. Alas, you can't cycle with a board under your arm but there's a decent surf school at Porthtowan you can hire one from instead.

COOL FACTOR Located on some of Cornwall's most popular cycling routes and with an excellent café to boot.

WHO'S IN Everyone! Campers, glampers, tents, campervans, motorhomes, caravans, dogs, groups.

ON SITE 20 grass pitches and 3 fully furnished bell tents. 2 compost toilets, 2 family-sized washroom cubicles with showers and sinks, and 2 dish-washing sinks. There's a flushing toilet and chemical disposal point beside the café (a short skip up the hill). Braziers and logs are provided for campfires (£5 per night). Bike hire is available at a reduced rate to campers, and is free for glampers.

OFF SITE Venture over the hill that shelters Elm Farm from the sea winds and you'll find the North Cornwall coastline waiting. It's a 30-minute walk to the cliffs. Nearby Portreath and Porthtowan each offer sandy coves, both great for surfing, with boards available for hire in the villages. Porthtowan is also blue-flag certified. The villages can be reached via the coast-to-coast cycle trail (sometimes called the Bissoe Trail) too or try various other local loops taking in the area's old mines – the Mineral Tramways network.

FOOD & DRINK Elm Farm Café offers a wide variety of refreshments, including Lavazza coffee, specialist teas, cakes, sandwiches, a superb all-day breakfast, light lunches and local ice-cream. It's also fully licensed, so expect Cornish real ale from Skinners Brewery and a glass of wine for the campfire. For anything else, pedal into Portreath and Porthtowan.

GETTING THERE Leave the A30 at Redruth turnoff and follow the road to Porthtowan. At the Chapel Hill T-junction, turn left and Elm Farm is 300 yards further on the right.

PUBLIC TRANSPORT Redruth train station (0845 748 4950) is 2 miles away. From there you can cycle or arrange a taxi.

OPEN April–October (glamping late May–September).

THE DAMAGE Adults £8–£10, children £4–£5, under-5s free. Dogs free. Bell tents (includes 2 people) £60–£75 per night.

Beacon Cottage Farm

Beacon Drive, St Agnes, Cornwall TR5 0NU   01872 552347   beaconcottagefarmholidays.co.uk

Cornwall offers the perfect seaside sojourn for any make or model of human holidaymaker: surf dudes and dudettes, sand fortress construction engineers (junior or senior), cute-village enthusiasts, ice-cream fans and suckers for scenery. All will find what they crave from a seaside break in England's south-west corner.

But Cornwall is not simply one place; its north and west fringes are very different from those on the south and east. The south of the county is sheltered, lush and lovely in a mild sort of way. With thatched villages nestling by wooded creeks among the green folds of the rolling countryside, it's many a gentlefolk's dream of the perfect holiday destination. The north coast, on the other hand, faces the full wrath of the Atlantic amid some of the wildest, roughest and most dramatic coastal scenery in Europe. This raw, windswept, surf-washed seaside is for many the very essence of Cornwall and this awesome location is where you'll find Beacon Cottage Farm.

That Beacon Cottage is knocked about by the wind in perhaps the rockiest, emptiest, and most beautiful section of Cornish coast just makes it even more impressive. The campsite itself is superb, with a choice of pitches either facing whatever the weather can throw at you – but with a stunning view – or sheltered from the elements in the orchard around the back of the farm. The facilities are top-notch and the proprietors – the Sawle family – are a warm and friendly lot. Choose between a pitch in the roomy Ocean View field or the more intimate orchard, which is closer to the facilities but doesn't have the views.

There is an eminently suitable beach nearby – indeed just 150 (very vertical) metres below the site. Also, less than a mile away along the coast path, Chapel Porth, with its immaculately wild looks and clean, unspoiled location, is one of the reasons Beacon Cottage is such a glam destination for young families in the school holidays. Ice-cream is provided from a stone hut in the small car park, but otherwise nothing else is allowed to ruin the beach's genuine USP which, to be honest, is much the same as that of the campsite – a remote position amid some of the most dramatic scenery in the land.

There's a historic and rather melancholic side to the place, too, one that's best discovered on foot. The former mining village of St Agnes is about two miles away from Beacon Cottage Farm along the coast path, which passes abandoned engine houses and mine shafts perched precariously on the cliffs along the way, before dropping into the rocky cleft of Trevaunance Cove. Here, in addition to the remnants of the industrial heritage, you'll find another decent family beach, clean surf and yet more locally made ice-cream for the kids (and hungry grown-ups too).

From the cove all roads lead back to Beacon Cottage, via possibly the most famous of Cornwall's picturesque derelict engine houses, at Wheal Coates Mine. For those who are suckers for scenery, and those who have that all-consuming passion to see it from inside their boots, this is a walker's Valhalla. How pleasing, then, that the campsite also has a special rate for backpackers and welcomes walkers of all stripes with open arms.

COOL FACTOR Slap bang in the middle of some of the most amazing – and historic – coastal scenery that the UK has to offer.

WHO'S IN Tents, campervans, motorhomes, caravans, dogs – yes. Groups – no.

ON SITE The level camping fields have hook-ups, with 43 of the total 70 pitches thus equipped. Some pitches are in an area with a spectacular sea view while others are in a landscaped area surrounded by trees for those who prefer some shelter. Facilities were refurbished in 2018, with toilets, showers (4 women's, 4 gent's), 3 family bathrooms and a laundry room. Washing-up sinks. Chemical disposal point. Ice packs, milk, eggs, gas and newspapers are sold at the farmhouse. No campfires, but BBQs off the ground are okay.

OFF SITE Chapel Porth beach is just 10–15 minutes' walk and is excellent for bathing and surfing and has lovely rock pools for children to play in. St Agnes village is 1½ miles' walk away, along footpaths – a lovely little country village with individual shops restaurants, pubs and quality craft shops. A 3-mile walk along the cliffs is Blue Hills Tin Streams (01872 553341), one of the few remaining working tin mines in the area, whose visitor centre gives some meaning to all the haunting ruins emblematic of this location, especially the coast around Beacon Cottage. Geevor Tin Mine (01736 788662) near St Just was a large-scale working mine until 1990, and these days the underground tour is the major attraction, while a café provides refreshment and the museum extra information. The delights of St Ives are just a short drive away and, on the way, at Hayle, the small zoo of Paradise Park (01736 753365) has a nice feel and makes a fantastic family day out. Those seeking cuddly cuteness will do no better than the National Seal Sanctuary

at Gweek, also to the south on the north edge of the Lizard peninsula, where they care for injured and orphaned seals from all over the UK, before releasing them back into the wild. Finally, the port of Falmouth on Cornwall's south coast is just half an hour away and also worth a visit – the waterfront National Maritime Museum (01326 313388) always proves a great hit with children of all ages.

FOOD & DRINK There are several decent places to eat and drink in St Agnes, including the St Agnes Hotel (01872 552307) on the main street, which offers a good selection of food and drink in a traditional-looking dining room at reasonable prices, and Taste (01872 552194), where they serve well-presented grub with a Mediterranean theme. Meanwhile, down in Trevaunance Combe (the valley leading to the Cove), the Driftwood Spars Hotel (01872 552428) not only has bar food and a restaurant with a large menu and good children's deals but its own brewery too. Try their selection of rustic ales – will it be Bolstor's Blood or a pint of Bawden Rocks? – or purchase a hamper to enjoy alongside your BBQ.

GETTING THERE Follow the A30 and, just past Blackwater, at the A390 roundabout, turn right on to the B3277 to St Agnes. On entering the village at the first mini-roundabout, take a sharp left into Goonvrea Road. Follow this for a mile and then turn right into Beacon Drive (following the caravan site signs). Beacon Cottage is on the right.

PUBLIC TRANSPORT Take a train to Cornwall's capital, Truro, from where there is a regular bus service (nos. 85 and 85A) to St Agnes.

OPEN Easter–end of September.

THE DAMAGE Tent plus 2 adults £19–£26, backpackers £9, children £3.50, dogs £3.

Treveague Farm

Gorran, Saint Austell, Cornwall PL26 6NY   01726 843467   treveaguefarm.co.uk

A family farm perched amid divine clifftop countryside and within easy reach of three sandy coves, Treveague Farm has everything a really good seaside campsite needs. So when you consider its extras – a café serving organic food, farm animals, a badger hide and an aviary with bantams, lovebirds and more – it really does notch up a few credits as a superb place to stay.

Spread across three meadows, with glorious sea views in two directions, this is the place to come for a proper coastal stay. When the wind blows it can be an exposed location, so you might want to opt for a space by the hedgerows rather than a front-row view. But the campsite's open setting really lends itself to families who want space to spread out and let the kids loose. Even with 100 pitches it's impossible to feel hemmed in here.

While kids gravitate to the farm animals, playground and storytelling sessions in the Secret Garden (great distractions when you want to chill out), make sure you tear them away from all this for a trip to the beach. After all, that's what this location is really all about and it's an easy stroll down to Hemmick Beach (though advisable to avoid the short-cut through a field of cattle if you have a dog in tow) and not much further to the clear blue waters of Vault Beach. The calf-grinding walk back up to camp is always a great excuse for a generous scoop of the Cornish ice-cream they serve in the campsite shop too.

COOL FACTOR Three beaches within reach, plus farm animals to pet and an excellent organic café.

WHO'S IN Tents, campervans, caravans, motorhomes, dogs – yes. Groups – no.

ON SITE 100 grass pitches, 40 with electric hook-ups. Facilities include indoor and outdoor sinks, fridges/freezers, laundry, babychanging and disabled access. Showers are 50p. Café and well-stocked campsite shop. Free Wi-Fi. Kids will love the playground and there are plenty of animals – pigs, cows and sheep – plus a wildlife hide for badger watching. No fires.

OFF SITE Of the beaches, Hemmick is the closest (10–15 minutes' walk) but Gorran Haven has more facilities and also boasts an ancient harbour and an excellent old pub. There's also the stunning Vault Beach, although this is a longer walk. Inland, you could explore the Lost Gardens of Heligan (01726 845100), which are a 10-minute drive away.

FOOD & DRINK There's little need to stray beyond the onsite café and restaurant but Gorran Haven's Barley Sheaf (01726 843330), the nearest pub, dating back to 1837, is well worth a visit. For a cuppa before your walk, try the Coast Path Café (07512 543735) or the Mermaid Beach Café (07971 886782), which is just as close to the footpath even if it doesn't boast the name.

GETTING THERE From St Austell take the B3273 to Mevagissey; past Pentewan, turn right at the crossroads at the top of the hill. Follow the signs to Heligan, then to Seaview campsite, and you'll see the signs to Treveague.

PUBLIC TRANSPORT Bus 526 from St Austell train station stops a 500m walk from the site.

OPEN Easter–end October.

THE DAMAGE A pitch and 2 people £8–£28. Extra people (5yrs+) £3. Under-5s free, dogs £3.

East Crinnis Farm

East Crinnis Holiday Park, East Crinnis, Par, Cornwall PL24 2SD   01726 813023   eastcrinnis.com

Ask 10 different campers to explain their favourite thing about East Crinnis Farm and you'll probably receive 10 different answers. Some like its peaceful rural setting, others might opt for the sparkly clean facilities, while a few may even choose the tasty Cornish pasties, served along with a night of storytelling round the campfire. Whichever aspect of this family-friendly campsite takes your fancy, you will undoubtedly enjoy this rustic retreat in the heart of Cornwall, where time seems to stand magnificently still.

The range of camping experiences on offer is pretty impressive. Traditionalists can pitch on one of the large, flat, grassy spaces, which are secluded by hedges. For those in search of creature comforts, log cabins and geodesic glamping domes are also available. The domes are situated in an exclusive area of the site (catching the best of the afternoon sun) and come equipped with log burners. What's more, a six-metre transparent section of wall allows for unimpeded star-gazing come nightfall.

Although this is essentially a rural location, East Crinnis is only a short jaunt away from the beaches, ice-cream kiosks and breathtaking scenery of the southern Cornish coast. It takes 45 minutes to wander the coastal path to Charleston Harbour (of the BBC's *Poldark* fame) following the high cliff edges above nearby Crinnis Beach, while cyclists will enjoy the moors and mineral trails inland. But it's not all about the Great Outdoors. The nearby traditional fishing ports of Mevagissey and Fowey both offer a pleasing variety of food and drink, activities and shopping, plus their very own summer festival season.

After a busy day discovering the ancient kingdom of Cornwall, switching off the car engine and winding down at East Crinnis is a joy. Despite the farm's wide range of facilities, the general ambience of this place is far away from the 'holiday park' vibe you might expect; as the night draws in, parents sweep up their offspring and head for a sing-song and snacks around the campfire. Glampers, meanwhile, head back to their geodesic cocoons to watch the skies in comfort. Whichever route you pick, this is camping as it should be, with a lovely atmosphere in a truly special location.

COOL FACTOR The family-friendly vibe, the postive encouragement of campfires and the extra glamping options.

WHO'S IN Tents, caravans, campervans, glampers, families and dogs (on a lead at all times) – yes.

ON SITE 40 level pitches, plus log cabins and geodesic domes. Facilities include showers, changing rooms, a family bathroom, babychanging room, hairdryers, disabled access, laundry room and a kitchen with freezers, kettle, microwave and washing-up facilities. Fresh water points around the campsite. Small shop selling essentials (see *Food & Drink*). Wi-Fi available. Children's play area, giant garden chess and a small nature reserve with a pond. Weekly storytelling around the campfire during school summer holidays.

OFF SITE A 15-minute walk takes you to the South West Coast Path, on the high cliffs above Crinnis beach. As well as nearby Fowey, the Cornish capital of Truro, the Lost Gardens of Heligan (01726 845100) and the Roseland Peninsula are also just half an hour away. Keen golfer? It's just a mile from East Crinnis Farm to Carlyon Bay Golf Course (01726 814250).

FOOD & DRINK A small shop on the campsite offers a 'shack' takeaway – expect the likes of locally sourced bacon, sausages, eggs and freshly baked bread for breakfast, with barista served coffee every morning, plus cold drinks and pasties in the evening. There are plenty of good places to eat in nearby Fowey, not least the award-winning restaurant of the Old Quay House hotel (01726 833302) and the welcoming and quirky Lifebuoy Café (07715 075869). Sam's (01726 832273) is a cool 1960s-style joint serving fish and famous burgers, with branches in both Fowey and on the beach in Polkerris.

GETTING THERE The site is half a mile from the A390. Take the Fowey turning by the Britannia Inn roundabout and follow the A3082; the campsite is on the left.

PUBLIC TRANSPORT Par railway station is 1¼ miles away. From there you can walk, cycle, or arrange a taxi.

OPEN March–October.

THE DAMAGE A pitch and 2 people from £11–£22. Extra campers £4 per person. See website for glamping prices.

Cerenety Eco Camping

Lower Lynstone Lane, Bude, Cornwall EX23 0LR   07429 016962   cerenetycampsite.co.uk

In the eyes of wild camping enthusiasts, campsites are for softies. But wild camping with kids – well, it can just be a bit of a hassle. At the very least it's nice to know there's running water to deal with potty mishaps and stacks of dirty dishes. With its no-frills, close-to-nature approach, Cerenety proves you can still enjoy the wilder side of camping on a regular campsite.

First and foremost, with the majority of the grassy fields left empty, even in the summer, Cerenety's seven sprawling acres mean there is plenty of space to run around like wild things. Every feature is as squeakygreen as the surrounding countryside, from compost loos and solar panels to recycled materials ingeniously put to use in the site's rustic, efficient amenities. There's even a veggie patch and a permaculture forest garden, where you can have a forage yourself and pick your own.

Children also flock to bottle-feed orphan lambs, and alpacas roam a few feet shy of the tents. Where nature rules and campfire smoke spirals lazily into dusky skies, it comes as a surprise that the surfer dudes, secret beaches and retro cafés of Bude are just a mile's easy stroll away along the canal. So kids can get a seaside fix without you having to hunt down the car keys. Once they've hit the waves, gorged on ice-cream, hired a pedalo or taken a dip in the tidal pool, you might even experience a rare moment of serenity when they rest their tired little heads back at camp.

COOL FACTOR Serene, green and very spacious. Even at full capacity there are just a handful of tents in each paddock.

WHO'S IN Couples, families, groups, small campervans, tents, dogs (by arrangement) – yes. Caravans, motorhomes – no.

ON SITE Three sprawling fields with no set pitches – just don't cramp your neighbours' style, and check with the owners which meadow to pitch in. A field shelter houses 2 showers, 3 compost loos and 2 washing-up sinks (hot water is powered by solar panels). Owner Jake will freeze ice-blocks for you in the house if you ask politely. A small shed-shop sells basics such as toothpaste and loo roll. Pick your own fresh veggies from the patch and explore the forest garden. Spot butterflies, moths and visiting herons on the wildlife pond. Feed the orphan lambs (in lambing season) and pet the animals – Flipper the dog, Torry the pony and Red the rescue horse, as well as alpacas, rabbits, ducks and chickens. Campfires and BBQs are not just permitted but very much encouraged.

OFF SITE It's a 50-minute walk to the campsite's 'secret beach' and a 20-minute stroll to Bude's stunning Summerleaze, Crooklets and Widemouth beaches, which serve up a heady cocktail of surf, sand, cool waterfront cafés and amusement arcades. Hit the waves with Raven Surf School (01288 353693) or Big Blue Surf School (01288 331764), or take a dip in the tidal pool. You can also enjoy some inland water by rowing a boat along the canal (boat hire at Lower Wharf: 07968 688782). Cyclists can opt for a gentle route along the canal towpath too.

FOOD & DRINK Walk to Bude for options. The nearest family-friendly pub is the Brendon Arms (01288 354542), ¾-mile away. Just beyond, the Olive Tree (01288 359577) offers Italian cuisine by the canal in a relaxed setting with a terrace, while across the river by Summerleaze beach, The Beach at Bude (01288 389800) has a restaurant and cool cocktail bar with a superb sea-facing terrace.

GETTING THERE Follow the signs for Bude. Once you arrive at the mini-roundabout where you would turn right for the town centre, go straight across towards Widemouth Bay. Follow the main road over the bridge, around to the left and up the hill. At the top of the hill you will see Upper Lynstone Caravan Park on the right side; turn left opposite here and follow the narrow lane to the end where you'll come to a T-junction. Turn right and the campsite is the first gate on the right, you'll probably see some animals and a small field shelter in the paddock. If you are coming from Widemouth, look out for signs from Cerenety on your right. Follow the winding road until you see Cerenety's campsite entrance.

PUBLIC TRANSPORT It's relatively easy to get to Cerenety using public transport. Take the train or bus to Exeter then get the bus (6 or 6A) from Exeter to Bude. From Plymouth it is also just a direct bus to Cerenety (12).

OPEN March–October.

THE DAMAGE Small tent £4–£5, large tent (6-person or more) £5–£8, Campervan £7–£10. Adults £4–£6, children (under 6yrs) £2. Car £2. Dogs £1–£2.

Fairlinch Camping

Saunton Road, Braunton, Devon EX33 1EB   07969 080873   fairlinch.co.uk

For most of the year there is little to see at Fairlinch. For 11 months the place operates as a traditional Devonshire farm and it is only from the last weekend in July to the first weekend of September that its metal gates are opened to campers, unveiling a small and simple slice of camping paradise to the general public.

Firstly, the Fairlinch field is fantastically spacious. Due to its impressive size, the meadow never feels overloaded and there is always plenty of space for ball games and family fun. Flat-as-a-pancake pitches are found at the ascending campsite's base or, if you don't mind sleeping on a wee slope, there's the reward of breathtaking coastal views from the summit.

The surrounding landscape can't fail to inspire, with the glorious and iconic Saunton Sands beach located just minutes away. Not content with being drop-dead gorgeous, Saunton Sands is also renowned for hosting some of Britain's finest surf conditions – when the Atlantic swell's good it produces row after row of slow rollers, proving irresistible for boarders.

Behind the beach, meanwhile, lies vast Braunton Burrows, England's largest psammosere (that's er... a sand dune system to you and me). Boasting an extraordinarily diverse plant community (with over 400 recorded species), its ecological importance has been recognised by UNESCO, ranking the site alongside Mount Vesuvius and the Danube Delta for international significance. Plus, credentials aside, it's a pretty great place for grown-ups and nippers alike to run wild and explore.

COOL FACTOR Moments away from surf-central Saunton Sands and the vast dune landscape of Braunton Burrows.

WHO'S IN Tents, caravans, campervans, sensible groups, motorcycles, gazebos (at no extra cost) and well-behaved dogs – yes.

ON SITE A large, ascending field (almost perfectly flat at the bottom) with room for 50 tent pitches and around 20 campervans or caravans. Ablution block with 6 electric showers, 2 toilet blocks and outdoor washing-up sinks. Mains drinking water, recycling point and reception hut. Campfires are permitted and logs are available at the local petrol station.

OFF SITE As well as the glory that is Saunton Sands, don't forget the beach – and village – at Croyde: a big surf dude spot in its own right. Book a local lesson with Surfing South West (01271 890400) or see how it all began with a visit to the Museum of British Surfing (01271 815155) in Braunton. You can also discover the area on 2 wheels via the renowned Tarka Trail – bikes can be hired from Otter Cycle Hire (01271 813339) in Braunton.

FOOD & DRINK It's a 10-minute walk to Braunton, where Squires (01271 815533) is an award-winning chippy that brings folk from miles around for both tasty takeaways and its sit-down restaurant. Surfer dudes (and dudettes), meanwhile, should make a beeline for The White Lion (01271 813085) for its rib-sticking burgers.

GETTING THERE From the traffic lights in Braunton town centre, follow the B3231 towards Croyde and Saunton. Fairlinch is a mile along the road (with a large sign) on the right.

PUBLIC TRANSPORT Bus services run from Barnstaple, with the 308 stopping at West Meadow Road (100m from the site). This bus also travels to Saunton and Croyde, allowing guests to visit the beach without having to pay parking costs.

OPEN End of July–start of September.

THE DAMAGE £10 per adult and £3 per child.

Ocean Pitch

Moor Lane, Croyde, Devon EX33 1NZ   07581024348   oceanpitch.co.uk

Thinking of Devon often evokes sepia-toned scenes of cream teas, chocolate-box cottages and rambling on wild Exmoor. Yet this genteel image of the county is only as true as you make it round these parts. Sure, there's the traditional Devonian charm of the sleepy village of Georgeham, not to mention the typical seaside 'candy-floss 'n' kiss-me-quick' delights of the family resort at Woolacombe. But if you've descended upon the North Devon coast with tent on back, board under arm and adventure on your mind, you've come to the right place – for Croyde is undoubtedly England's surf capital.

Acres of sand, pounding surf, and bronzed lifeguards... welcome to the Gold Coast. It may be a tad cooler than the Aussie version but, more importantly, it is much nearer for us Poms. Okay, so our cousins down under might enjoy near perma-sunny skies, but on an early summer morning, with the breeze just right, we'd take Croyde over Byron Bay any day of the week. With its lush green hills ravining down to blustery expanses of open beach, there's no disputing the beauty of Croyde Bay. This wide sweep of dune-backed sand flanked by the finest field-green North Devon hills is the closest thing you'll find to an Aussie surf beach in this part of the world, gifting awesome waves to both pros and beginners.

Former visitors lucky enough to have secured a pitch at legendary local campsite Mitchum's will know all about the spectacular views from this enviably elevated spot. In latter years, however, the campsite has been operating under the name Ocean Pitch – and newbies and veterans alike will be pleased to know that surfing still features high on the agenda.

As wonderful new owners Benny and Lou are all too aware, surfers are an enthusiastic bunch; hours can pass as they scan the endless blue horizon for that elusive perfect wave. But from its priceless vantage point, Ocean Pitch is one of the few campsites in the area with direct beach views, meaning you can keep an eye on the surf from your... erm... ocean pitch, and race down with your board when the waves are breaking. And if you're not here for the surf, it's just as great being able to wake up and see the ocean each morning as you cook your breakfast sausages. Stunning Croyde Bay provides a perfect canvas for this unparalleled campsite masterpiece and the site is on the coastal path, so it's easy to reach the neighbouring beaches on foot.

COOL FACTOR Stunning views over Croyde Bay and instant beach access.

WHO'S IN Tents, campervans, couples, families – yes. Young groups and family groups with lots of children – check in advance. Caravans, dogs, stags and hens – no.

ON SITE 40 pitches all with views of Croyde Beach and the ocean (just 5 with electrical hook-ups available), plus 3 glamping pods. Hot showers, immaculately clean toilets, outside cold showers for washing wetsuits, outside washing-up basins, basic tent hire, Wi-Fi internet access, BBQ bricks, mobile phone/tablet battery charging at reception, onsite snack shack, friendly staff on site 24hrs.

OFF SITE Book lessons onsite with Surf South West (01271 890400) or take advantage of the stunning heritage coastline path with a walk to Baggy Point. Croyde Bay also hosts the annual Oceanfest (01271 817000) – a beach, sports and music festival in June. Horseriding on Croyde beach is a must-do experience, whether a leisurely beach trot or epic country trek, and the family-run Roylands Riding Holidays (01271 890898) in central Croyde welcomes experienced riders and first-timers all year round.

FOOD & DRINK You can buy cold drinks and chocolate bars onsite, plus Ocean Pitch have a cool retro slush puppy machine. Ivan's cool coffee-serving campervan also parks up during peak season. Elsewhere, scoff a Devon cream tea at Centery Farm (01271 879603) or try The Thatch pub (01271 890349), a lively surfers' hangout with decent food. The Blue

Groove (01271 890111) combines laid-back beach-bum vibe with trippy artwork and an internationally eclectic menu that includes Thai curries, Mexican pancakes and Japanese noodles. In the village of Georgeham, just inland, try the more traditional food and real ales at The Rock Inn (01271 890322), where they do a great Sunday lunch and serve lunch and dinner daily in a light, bright conservatory. Find out more about organic farming and conservation at the dairy at West Hill Farm (01271 815477) and taste their wares.

GETTING THERE Ocean Pitch is the closest campsite to the beach in Croyde. Coming into Croyde, drive through the village and turn left on to Moor Lane towards the beach. Drive ½ mile down this road until the beach is on your left-hand side and Ocean Pitch Campsite is the last field on your right – there are clear signs outside.

PUBLIC TRANSPORT From Barnstaple train station walk the 10 minutes to the bus station and take bus 308 to Moor Lane, Croyde. Benny and Lou can do shuttle run collections/drop-offs for a small fee (maximum of 4 people; arrange well in advance). Alternatively, call Saunton Taxis (07890 543136) for the best local price.

OPEN Easter–mid September.

THE DAMAGE Adults £15, children (3–15yrs) £7.50; bookings for under-3s not permitted. Cars £3 per night. Pods from £99 per night. Surfboard hire £12 per day (£16 with wetsuit); body board hire £8 per day (£13 with wetsuit); separate wetsuit hire £8 per day; SUP hire £25 per half day or £40 per full day.

Little Meadow

Watermouth, Ilfracombe, Devon EX34 9SJ 01271 862222 littlemeadow.co.uk

The ancient South American tribes of Inca and Maya might have invented terracing to help with their crop cultivation, but seldom can they have done it as well as the folk have here at Little Meadow. By levelling off the land in a series of flat lawns they've ensured that campers benefit from being plumb-line level with the well-tended soft grass for easy tent pegging while still enjoying views of the stunning North Devon coast. This Area of Outstanding Natural Beauty has everything: dramatic cliffs, wide sandy beaches and quaint little coves and harbours.

The terracing also helps create privacy – you'd never guess there are 50 pitches on this unassuming, environmentally friendly campsite, all part of a beautifully kept 100-acre organic farm. Part of this is down to their sensible policy on dwelling size, with the campsite owners actively discouraging mega-size tents or massive motorhomes. Everywhere you walk brings another unexpected delight, whether it's a rabbit hip-hopping across a nearby meadow or a set of swings for kids tucked away in a corner. There's also an outdoor table tennis table set up for use by all guests, and you can buy bats and balls at reception. While here, why not pick up some of the store's lovely regional products – from bacon, eggs and local meats to truly moreish homemade cakes? Bright splashes of flowers border the pitching areas, providing colourful framing to the views over Watermouth Bay, the Bristol Channel and the cliffs of Hangman Point. Its proximity to all things nautical is also in evidence, with huge old anchors, carved driftwood and colourful floats and buoys scattered around the reception area. It's a magnificent spot in which to settle comfortably into a deckchair, or one of the giant hammocks, and survey the scenery – you might even spy a seal or a basking shark if you're lucky (and in possession of a good pair of binoculars).

If you can drag yourself away, though, there are several must-dos in the area. A day trip to Lundy Island, by ferry from nearby Ilfracombe, offers outstanding views of England, Wales and the Atlantic. It might be just 11 miles from the mainland, but the sense of remoteness is incredible. There's no ferry between November and March, but well-heeled folk can always opt for the daily helicopter service (Mon–Fri). You should also consider taking a fishing trip from Ilfracombe to catch bass, pollack, whiting, cod and mackerel, which are all plentiful here. Gut them on the boat and you could have your breakfast, lunch and dinner sorted for the day. Alternatively, spend a day learning to ride the waves at one of the many surf schools in the area, at Woolacombe, Croyde or Saunton Sands; while nearby Exmoor is fabulous for walking. For the best routes, it's not far from the campsite to The Hunter's Inn pub, from where there are any number of glorious treks you could do, including an easy stroll to the sea at Heddon's Mouth. With excellent views and a cracking seaside finish, it's the perfect way to earn yourself a pint at the pub afterwards.

COOL FACTOR Well-tended terraces providing magnificent ocean views.

WHO'S IN Tents, campervans, caravans, dogs (on leads) – yes. Groups, mega-size tents and huge motorhomes – no.

ON SITE Approximately 50 pitches (draughty in high winds), plus an octagonal wooden pod for glampers. The wash-block has toilets (disabled access), hot showers, a washing machine and hairdryers. There's also ice-pack freezing and a basic shop selling essentials, fresh organic milk, homemade cakes and local farm meats. Hook-ups are available. There's a small, wooded play area for kids, as well as table tennis, Wi-Fi and a dog-exercising area. Campfires not permitted.

OFF SITE The closest attraction to the site is Watermouth Castle (01271 867474), a large stately home with old-fashioned exhibitions inside and a theme park behind – good fun for small children. Just the other side of the nearby seaside village of Combe Martin, the Combe Martin Wildlife and Dinosaur Park (01271 882486) is a zoo-cum-theme park with a dinosaur slant – including some splendid animatronic creatures alongside seals, monkeys, a spot of falconry and whatever else they have been able to squeeze in. In the opposite direction you can explore the rockpools at the unique Victorian Tunnels Beaches in Ilfracombe (01271 879882) and enjoy the landscaped seafront nearby, with its Landmark Theatre, which doubles as the local information centre. Ilfracombe also has a couple of museums that are worth visiting on rainy days – the Ilfracombe Town Museum, on the seafront (01271 863541) and a small aquarium in the harbour (01271 864533), not to mention the long-standing Ilfracombe Chocolate Emporium (01271 867193), which makes and sells its own chocolates and sweets. For a beautiful, tucked-away coastal spot, check out Barricane Beach at nearby Woolacombe, a lovely inlet that is the final destination for millions of small shells that are whisked here from the Caribbean. Woolacombe Beach itself is a beautiful spot, whether you are surfing or just beach-lounging – the latter best done at its far end, where Putsborough Beach has a lovely café overlooking the sea.

FOOD & DRINK The onsite shop sells milk, cheese, eggs and homemade cakes. For a real culinary treat why not try La Gendarmerie (01271 865984)? Gazpacho (01271 862545) offers fabulously authentic paella cooked by a Spanish chef; Espresso (01271 855485) is a seafood restaurant famous for its crab and lobster dishes – all caught locally – while Brit-art wonderboy Damien Hirst's Number 11 The Quay (01271 868090) flies the flag for modern British cuisine and has great sea views from its main dining room as well as a convivial downstairs bar with outside tables. Try also the renowned Sri Lankan curry shack pitched on the edge of the sand at Barricane Beach during the summer months. There's not much in Combe Martin itself, although the large Pack o' Cards pub (01271 882300), halfway up the long High Street (Britain's longest, in fact), does pub grub and has a nice beer garden with lots of activities for kids. Closer to the campsite – within walking distance – The Old Sawmill Inn (01271 882259) is a perfectly serviceable family pub located down the hill near Watermouth Bay.

GETTING THERE Little Meadow lies between Ilfracombe and Combe Martin. It's about an hour from the M5; leave at J27, take the A361 to Barnstaple. Just past the South Molton exit, turn right to Allercross roundabout (signposted Combe Martin). Go through Combe Martin and the campsite can be found on the right.

PUBLIC TRANSPORT Travel to Barnstaple on the train, then catch the 301 bus (to Combe Martin). There's a bus stop at the campsite's entrance, just before Watermouth Castle stop.

OPEN Easter–late September.

THE DAMAGE Tent, 2 people and a car £14.50–£20 per night.

Caffyns Farm

Lynton, Devon EX35 6JW   01598 753967   exmoorcoastholidays.co.uk

After a successful reign running another *Cool Camping* recommended site, Cloud Farm, Colin and Jill Harman have upped sticks and moved to a new and more breathtaking location; this time with sea views, open fields and endless space on the North Devon coast.

When they arrived at Caffyns Farm, the Harmans brought with them their trove of cool campsite know-how and, alongside the farm's family B&B and a superb new café, have been busy creating a relaxed, rule-free, pitch-wherever-you-fancy campsite. A campfire culture is encouraged and is even more magical given the location – surrounded by expansive countryside and views over the Bristol Channel that spread endlessly beyond your flickering flames.

Campers are free to wander over any of the 150 acres of farmland, which is some of the flattest in this undulating area of Exmoor – all the better for pitching. So far there are four camping fields edged by protective hedgerows, but there are plans to open up more; a couple of which will be adorned by a yurt or two for glamping. And this is just a fraction of what the Harmans have in store for Caffyns Farm.

Even if it takes a while for their dream site to be completed, this campsite is a cracker as it is. The location is beautiful and the laid-back vibe ensures friendly, relaxed campers. It's an irresistible spot for kids who are hooked on riding and beach days, too, with pony-trekking right from the farm's own stables and walks down to the stunning beach at Lee Bay for days spent bodyboarding, sandcastle-building and rock pooling.

COOL FACTOR Lots of space in gorgeous surroundings – plus friendly ponies to ride.

WHO'S IN Tents, small campervans, dogs – yes. Groups – by prior arrangement. Caravans and large motorhomes – no.

ON SITE Multiple meadows, water standpipes in each. Facilities block has 8 showers, 16 loos, a disabled toilet, family shower room, laundry, fridge, freezer, microwaves and washing-up sinks. Bikes available for hire. They have over 30 ponies, so you can go off trekking to your heart's content (£25 per hour; age 5+). Excellent shop and tearoom in a converted barn space, plus a family B&B if the weather is truly terrible!

OFF SITE Walk directly from the farm down the steep coastal pathways to Lee Abbey and on down to the private beach (better to drive if you have very little children as the terrain's not buggy friendly). The beach has big, grey rocks for playing giant stepping stones with little pools in between for crabbing. The waves are high enough for bodyboarding but low enough for swimming. Down the coast a few miles, take a trip on The Cliff Railway (a funicular really), between Lynmouth and Lynton (01598 753486) and gape at the scenery before stopping for ice-cream at The Cliff Top café at the top.

FOOD & DRINK Jill's cakes are to die for. Find them all in the brand new tearoom and café, set in one of the farm's converted barns (complete with beams and adjoining garden with sea views) along with breakfasts, light lunches, coffees, soft and alcoholic drinks, snacks, baguettes and other refreshments. The café also has plenty of helpful info about Exmoor and the area.

GETTING THERE Take the A39 coast road west to Barbrook. Continue for a further mile and you'll see a sign for Caffyns Cross; turn right and continue up the lane, ignoring the first campsite, until you reach Caffyns Farm.

OPEN March–end of October.

THE DAMAGE Adults £8.50, children (5–15yrs) £7, under-5s camp for free.

Karrageen

Bolberry, Malborough, Kingsbridge, Devon TQ7 3EN   01548 561230   karrageen.co.uk

Karrageen is all about giving its lucky occupants – young and slightly less young – plenty of room to breathe, think, play and relax. There will be no tangle of guy ropes here, and there's even room for those multi-bedroom monstrosities that can take up a good few pitches on their own. If you want to do some proverbial cat-swinging there are few better camping patches in Devon.

It may well be that the abundance of space is allowed by the lack of all other things. You'll find nothing fancy, nothing flash and nothing gimmicky here: just a simple, very well-maintained and nicely landscaped campsite in an ever-so-lovely location – with extra room to spare.

The immediate locality of Karrageen is very peaceful, accessed along a single-track Devon lane (with plenty of passing places) leading down to the sea at the lost world of Hope Cove and its little village. After wandering through the sleepy rows of fishermen's cottages you'll think it eminently possible that this is still a place of clandestine meetings of pirates and smugglers, and that a raid from 'the revenue' isn't far off – such is the sense of detachment and timelessness in the air. If you fancy breakfast by your tent, why not devour one of Karrageen's locally renowned fresh croissants and *pain au chocolats*? There are a couple of pubs in the village serving decent food too. So there's little need to stray far during your stay and, no doubt, very little desire to either.

COOL FACTOR Space for families to spread out and relax.

WHO'S IN Tents, campervans, caravans, dogs – yes. Groups – no.

ON SITE The camping field is a terraced hillside split into a series of quite small, intimate and attractive cul-de-sacs where no one overlooks anyone else. Pitches are large and many have views across the valley. Plenty of electrical hook-ups. Facilities are excellent, with loos and 9 showers (4 women, 4 men, 1 family/disabled room equipped for babychanging). The 20p shower charge is to preserve Karrageen's scarce spring-water supply. There are 50 hook-ups, and campers have access to the freezer. Downsides: some static caravans lurking about; no campfires, though BBQs off the ground are okay.

OFF SITE All the attractions of south Devon are easily accessible from here, but locally – aside from walking the cliff paths – the boat trips on the rivers are the real treats: book a return sailing trip from Kingsbridge to Salcombe (01548 853607) or a River Dart trip from Totnes to Dartmouth (01803 555872). Alternatively, head down the coast a little way to Bigbury-on-Sea and walk or take the sea tractor across to Burgh Island.

FOOD & DRINK Posh nosh with a view can be found at The South Sands Hotel (01548 859000) in Salcombe, while in Hope itself The Sun Bay Hotel (01548 561371) does very good food. Also overlooking Hope Cove, The Hope and Anchor (01548 561295) offers pub-grub favourites at pleasing prices.

GETTING THERE From the A38 at Wrangaton take the A3121 south;turn left on to the B3196 to Kingsbridge and then the A381 towards Salcombe. After 3 miles take the second turn to Hope Cove and Bolberry; the site is 2 miles further on.

OPEN Easter–end of September.

THE DAMAGE Tent, car, plus 2 adults and 2 children £17–£34 per night. Electricity £3. Dogs £1–£2.

Beryl's Campsite

Beeson, Kingsbridge, Devon TQ7 2HW   07967 116682   berylscampsite.co.uk

The only clue to this campsite's existence is a hand-branded 'camping' sign nestled in a flowerbed. The site, which originally had no name and was known by locals simply as 'the one run by Beryl', has now been officially christened Beryl's by the campers themselves. The friendly lady in question describes the secretive site, hidden at the end of a tunnel of trees in Beeson village, as her 'unconventional camping haven'. Charming eccentricity is certainly apparent here, not only in the laissez-faire attitude to publicity, but also in the quirky names of the 29 pitches, such as 'Panoramic' and 'Snug'.

The 'haven' part of Beryl's description is equally apt for this lush little site, nestled as it is on a hill in the woods with a glorious view of Start Bay. Venture down the narrow access road – even the rarely accepted caravan has been known to brave it – and you're rewarded with a real sanctuary from which to explore the surrounding delights of the Devonshire coast. You can spy on birds from the hide looking over the local nature reserve's lake, watch sailing boats silently move across the glistening bay, or take a walk around Slapton Ley lagoon just over the hill. The South West Coast Path is also easily reached, passing the award-winning beach at Beesands, just below the campsite.

COOL FACTOR A secret, secluded campsite with wonderful views down to the sea.

WHO'S IN Tents, campervans, dogs – yes. Caravans – no. Groups – by arrangement only.

ON SITE 20+ pitches over 7 grassy paddocks (hook-ups are available on a few pitches). Good facilities, with recycling bins, fridges, freezers, toilets, showers (coin-operated, 20p), washing-up sinks, and power points for charging mobiles. Campfires permitted but must be raised off the grass (firepits and logs available to hire). Woodland walks around the forest – get up early enough and you may even see some deer. There's plenty of space to play ball games and for some quiet contemplation.

OFF SITE Beesands (a 5–10 minute walk away) is the nearest of the many beaches nearby and the campsite is right on the South West Coast Path. If you like to explore there are several smaller quiet coves, too, just ask onsite for the most secretive spots that even we won't spill the beans on. If you fancy a day away from the beach, the local towns of Salcombe, Kingsbridge, Totnes and Dartmouth are all within a 30-minute drive, and for the kids there's the Woodlands Theme Park (01803 712598) – a great option if the weather turns grey. Mediterranean-like Blackpool Sands bay and its secret gardens are well worth a visit too on a sunnier day.

FOOD & DRINK In Beesands, the best place to eat by far is the fab Cricket Inn (01548 580215), famous for its seafood pancake and much else besides. Britannia @ The Beach (01548 581168) is a small 'shack' restaurant with a takeaway hatch. If you like cake, every Sunday St Andrews Church in Beesands sells drinks and cake (all homemade and with much of the money raised going straight to charity or to the church). Over the hill in Torcross, the Startbay Inn (01548 580553) is also renowned for its seafood dishes, and The Boat House (01548 580747) serves excellent pizzas and more.

GETTING THERE From the A379 either coming from Kingsbridge (east) or Dartmouth (west), turn off at a small roundabout when you get to the village of Stokenham and the signposts to Beesands. Follow the road for about 2 miles until you reach a left-hand T-junction where a sign points to Beeson/Beesands. Follow this road for another ¼ mile until you see the sign for Beeson. Continue to follow the road around a left bend and on the next right bend, in front of you, there is a wooden 'Camping' sign which directs you to the campsite.

PUBLIC TRANSPORT Buses usually run every hour during the day along the A379 from Kingsbridge to Dartmouth and back – Stokenham is the nearest stop but from there it is still almost 2 miles to the campsite.

OPEN Late April–late September (weather dependent).

THE DAMAGE A pitch and 4 people £24–£28. Extra adults £8, children (4–16yrs) £4 and under-4s £1. Electrical hook-ups £4 per night.

Beach Games

There's more to the beach than just sunbathing and swimming; keep the kids entertained with these handy game suggestions.

Taking your tots on a camping trip? We love family camping – we've even written entire guidebooks dedicated to it – and, when it comes to the coast there's no finer way to pass the day than frolicking right beside the sea.

Sandy beaches are practically designed for rough and tumble games – the surface is cushiony soft, wonderfully flat and offers a ready-made crashmat, yet it's still firm enough for fearsome games of beach cricket, football, volleyball or rounders.

But, while you can load the car with bats and balls, buckets and spades, surfboards and scooters, there's also plenty of fun to be had without filling your wagon to the rafters with equipment. Sometimes the best beach games are discovered when you come armed with only your imagination.

Often, the sand itself can provide the entertainment: why not sculpt a mermaid, bury a family member or simply dig a ginormous hole? Sand isn't the only natural plaything either – collecting shells and skimming stones into the breakers can entertain all ages for hours.

To help get your own ideas off the ground, we've picked out just a few suggestions that require little or no equipment other than the things you can find around you (or might naturally have in your bag).

Try a few of our favourite games and then adapt them even further, creating weekend-long championships and multiple round competitions. Whether you're in a big group or just heading to the beach as a family, there's endless fun to be had.

Sandcastle Competition

Building a sandcastle is hardly a new idea but there's a reason it's stood the test of time. Make the age-old tradition into a competition by challenging game players to take on the task of building the very best fortress. Draw equally-sized spaces in the sand for each player and set out any rules (like whether buckets are allowed or if decorations must be natural), then set a time limit and declare the competition open. If you've got buckets, fantastic, but if not, you can freestyle it, moulding with your hands and decorating with shells, stones and driftwood. Team up an adult with a child, go head-to-head or sit back, relax and let the kids quietly beaver away until the serious business of judging starts.

Sharks & Minnows

Mark out a large rectangular playing area in the sand by drawing with a stick or using jumpers for markers – the size depends on the number of people, but five large paces by fifteen is a good start. One person is appointed as the Shark and stands in the centre of the playing area. Everyone else, the Minnows, goes to one end and the Shark begins the game. It's tradition to shout: "Fishy, fishy cross my ocean", but feel free to make up your very own war cry. At this point all the Minnows try to cross the shark-infested waters without being caught. Anyone who is tagged becomes a Shark. Those who successfully make it to the end are safe – until the Shark tempts them back across the ocean once again. The winner is the last Minnow caught (who becomes the first Shark for the next round).

Beachcombers' Hunt

Make the absorbing activity of combing the shoreline into a competitive sport by declaring it a scavenger hunt. If you're organised you could write a list before you arrive and hand it out to your beach-combing competitors but it's possible, perhaps even preferable, to come up with a list on location after you've had a scout about at the flotsam and jetsam on the shoreline. If your hunters are young you may want to set out a defined search area so no one goes wandering off too far in pursuit of their treasure but otherwise it's a simple case of listing the items you want them to collect and letting them loose on the beach. Items might include a stone with a hole in it, a stick of driftwood, a piece of glass that's been smoothed by the sea or a particular type of shell. The first to return with all their items wins.

Water Relay Race

As long as you've got a couple of buckets (or even ice-cream tubs) and a cup or two from your picnic, you'll be able to organise a water relay. Divide the players into two teams and draw a line in the sand parallel to, but some distance from, the shoreline. Place two buckets on the side of the line furthest from the water and form your two teams up alongside them in two orderly queues. Give the first person in each line a small cup, then start the race. The aim of the game is, one by one, for each team member to run to the sea and fill a cup, running back to the bucket while retaining as much water as possible. The object of the exercise is to fill the bucket so, be warned, it can take a while!

Shells & Stones

Better known as noughts and crosses or tic-tac-toe, Shells and Stones follows the same principles but with objects from the beach. A quieter game that's suitable for two players, it can last from a couple of minutes to several hours if you play multiple games and keep score. Stage one involves challenging your competitors to find the pieces they are going to play with. Allocate one player as Shells and one as Stones, then send them off to find five of each of their namesake pieces. Once the search is complete, draw a noughts and crosses-style grid in the sand, then take it in turns to place your shells and stones in each of the squares with the aim of getting three in a row.

Limbo

This party favourite needs little explanation: essentially two people hold a rope, bar, stick or tent pole at shoulder height and the limbo competitors try to shimmy underneath, with feet facing forwards and back arched behind. Touch the bar and you're out, get under and you can stay for the next round when the bar is lowered and you have to contort your body further to get underneath. The beach is probably the best place to try it since, if you're playing on powdery sand, you're unlikely to do yourself an injury when you eventually fall over. Both adults and children can compete against one another in this game. And, as a well-known classic, you can almost guarantee that even the most sticky stick-in-the-mud will join the orderly queue to see just how low they can go.

Hook Farm

Gore Lane, Uplyme, Lyme Regis, Dorset DT7 3UU   01297 442801   hookfarmcamping.com

Island-hopping dinosaurs were part of the scenery in these parts some 190 million years ago. Many lost their footing and fell into the sea, leaving their mark on what became known as the Jurassic Coast. Hunting down their fossils is a popular sport in the quaint harbour resort of Lyme Regis.

Picturesque and peaceful but within a stone's throw of the lively harbour town, Hook Farm offers the best of both rural and urban worlds. Tucked away in the small village of Uplyme, with views up the pretty Lym Valley, it's a lovely, leafy site that feels quite remote: being in a designated 'Dark Valley' there's no light pollution at night, so just lie back and watch the stars emerge on a clear evening.

A few steps is all it takes to be warmly welcomed at reception, whisked past a section for caravans, and ushered into a beautiful terraced garden valley, where campers look like they're proudly privy to one of the best-kept camping secrets on the south coast.

The site itself is well maintained and welcoming, with pitches on several different levels, some spacious and open, others secluded and sheltered behind trees and bushes. All offer ample room to spread out with gazebos and blankets if needed, while a dozen are tucked beside various bushy nooks and crannies, offering the most privacy on the campsite. You could select your patch according to your sleeping habits. Early risers should head west to enjoy the morning sun, while night owls looking for a lie-in can camp to the east, where the last rays of the day fall. Sunsets look best from the top of the hill, and the lower area is better shielded from the elements.

Friendly, quiet and gently undulating, it's a perfect spot for families: children will enjoy the playground, complete with an old boat to clamber around upon, while their parents may appreciate the well-stocked shop selling fresh bread and croissants in the mornings and the village pub within easy strolling distance that serves local real ales and wholesome pub grub.

And if the peace and quiet of the countryside isn't enough for you, there's a cracking 45-minute walk down the valley which runs alongside the River Lym and into the cobbled backstreets and alleyways of Lyme Regis, with its bustling harbour, arty gift shops, sandy beach and array of restaurants and cafés. You can either make it a circular walk and return via the coastal path (the camp shop can provide details of the walking route and maps) or, if you can't face the steep walk back uphill, call the resident local taxi, which will come and pick you up and take you back to the campsite for around about a fiver.

Fortunately for any young, eager fossil-hunters returning empty-handed from a day's beachcombing, plastic dinosaur eggs are sold in the campsite shop. These ought to lift spirits before the next outing.

COOL FACTOR An attractive terraced site in a prime location for both fossil-hunting and the seaside resort of Lyme Regis.

WHO'S IN Tents, campervans, caravans, dogs (only certain breeds), families – yes. Groups – by prior arrangement only.

ON SITE 100 spacious tent pitches (58 with hook-ups), and 17 static caravans. Large, clean toilet blocks with solar-powered showers, freezers, a washing machine and dryer. Children's playground and a well-stocked shop selling local meat and eggs. Campfires are not permitted but BBQs are okay as long as they are raised off the ground.

OFF SITE Guided 3-hour fossil walks along the coastline (Sat–Tues only; 07854 377519). The Dinosaurland Fossil Museum in Lyme Regis (01297 443541) opens daily. There are great walks down the valley to Lyme Regis and along the coastal path; fossil-hunting beneath the local cliffs; and exploring the shops, cafés and restaurants of Lyme Regis. Oh, and if the weather's good, you can just go to the beach.

FOOD & DRINK Hugh Fearnley-Whittingstall's River Cottage (01297 630302) is less than 2 miles away. Or take your pick of the many places in Lyme Regis, from Thai on the seafront at Largigi (01297 442432) to high-end cuisine at Hix Oyster & Fish House (01297 446910), where floor-to-ceiling windows giving breathtaking views over the harbour and Cobb.

GETTING THERE From Axminster head south on the A35 then right on to the B3165 (Lyme Road). In Uplyme, turn right opposite the Talbot Arms pub into Gore Lane; the campsite's on the right.

PUBLIC TRANSPORT Train to Axminster, Dorchester, or Weymouth, then bus 31 to the Talbot Arms stop, and up the steep hill to the site.

OPEN March–October half-term.

THE DAMAGE Tent plus 2 adults £15–£35 (depending on season and tent size) per night; children (5–16yrs) £2.50, under-5s free. Electric hook-ups £3.50.

Eweleaze Farm

Osmington, Weymouth, Dorset DT3 6ED   01305 833690   eweleaze.co.uk

Eweleaze is the Glastonbury Festival of UK campsites. Advance tickets sell out shortly after going on sale; resident cows are herded into other, temporary, grassy accommodation; the production is super-slick; and food and drink is available in abundance. The capacity is the largest in the UK, too; over a thousand people a day share this clifftop location. And, like Glastonbury, its faithful fans return every year, won over by a curving Jurassic coastline that's cherry-topped with its own private, shingle beach. A steep, dusty track leads down to the camping village. In daylight, the sight of all the fields looks quite, quite special. At night, it's downright magical, lit up with campfires and twinkling fairy lights. Collect car passes at reception – stopping perhaps at the courtyard where there is a well-stocked shop, a popular bakery, solar-powered showers, puppies and roaming goats, geese, peacocks and pigs – before searching for a camping spot.

The Beach field is unsurprisingly closest to the steps that lead to the beach and the small pontoon (a big hit among the kids). The Track field is further from the sea and facilities, but you can keep your vehicle by your pitch. The Point field is quieter, but can be windy at night. It can take a few seasons to master your own personal preference.

A 'no music policy', except on Saturdays, is the main difference between Eweleaze and Glastonbury. In fact, groups wishing to gas all night should head for the back fields where there is more privacy. The main demographic is young, urban families who need a good night's sleep before their cherubs wake up in the morning. There are lots of regulars who know the drill and it's easy to see why they keep on coming back.

COOL FACTOR Loads of space, great views, a private beach and campfires. Cracking.

WHO'S IN Tents, campervans, caravans, dogs, groups – yes.

ON SITE Around 400 unmarked pitches over 8 fields, plus bell tents to hire; 33 showers – 8 outdoor solar-powered; toilets in each field; firewood and hay bales (for sitting and playing on); access to private beach with pontoon. As well as the bakery, there are pizza and ice-cream huts. A shop (8am–9pm) sells food, drinks, gas, kites, camping and snorkelling gear, and has a mobile charging service (£1 per visit). Campfires permitted.

OFF SITE The South West Coast Path follows the coastline in both directions from the campsite; the stretch from Durdle Door to Weymouth is particularly rewarding. The latter is a great spot for sailing; SailLaser (0845 337 3214) offer various courses from £150, or you can hire a boat if you're already qualified. For a family day-trip, Monkey World (01929 462537) in Bovington (11 miles) is worth a visit and is just down the road from the excellent Tank Museum (01929 405096), while Dorchester (5 miles) also has a heap of good museums.

FOOD & DRINK Sleep in and send the kids to the bakery to pick up the *pain au chocolats*. Tea and coffee is decaf only (owner, Pete, believes the world doesn't need caffeine, but he's created a camping utopia, so we'll forgive him). Woodfire pizzas (served midday–8pm) are small but tasty. The onsite farm shop (8am–9pm) sells organic meats, along with fresh doughnuts, burgers, pies and the perennial tea-time favourite, marshmallows. Osmington's Smugglers Inn (01305 833125) is a view-tastic 40-minute walk along the coast path.

GETTING THERE From the east, take the A35 towards Dorchester, then the B3390 and A353 to Osmington. After the village, look out for a speed-limit sign, and turn left here. From the west on the A353, continue through Preston, look out for the speed-limit sign just before Osmington, and turn right.

PUBLIC TRANSPORT The 503 bus from Weymouth stops at Waterside Holiday Park, a 300m walk away.

OPEN End July–end August.

THE DAMAGE Adults £9/£18 (weeknight/weekend-night), children (3–14yrs) £4.50/£9, under-3s free. Vehicles £15 flat fee.

Muddycreek Farm

Lymington Road, New Forest, Milford on Sea, Hampshire SO41 0RF 01590 681882   muddycreekfarm.co.uk

Hurst Castle is not your archetypal fort-shaped building. Thanks to the Napoleonic wars it has long, weird-looking flanks that bend around the coast. Its centre is still the rotund stone castle that Henry VIII commissioned, though, sitting like a circular watch face in the middle of two enormous granite straps. The castle's shape mirrors the curvature of the spit on which it resides, an outlying strip of shingle that runs in to Milford on Sea. And it's on the other side of this village that Muddycreek Farm resides.

Like the castle, Muddycreek Farm has been here for years and, while much of the countryside has been developed, the fields here remain largely untouched, the countryside a patchwork of agricultural colours. The perfect setting, then, for a campsite, and a pop-up one at that – a tent-only haven that drops into existence for 28 days of the year before returning back to nature.

Muddycreek Farm is a campsite that gets it right. There's no swimming pool, no laundry blocks, no strings of static caravans. In fact, if you came here in mid September you'd never even know the site existed. Yet at the height of August the 60 pitches each harbour a colourful tent, enlivened by the quiet hum of satisfied campers and kids yawning in their sleepbags. "Hmmm... 60-odd tents?!", you say? It may sound a little full, but with an expansive 15 acres of space there's no such problem here. Peg down in the soft grass and fold out your tables and chairs; there's no danger of feeling hemmed in by other peoples' guy ropes.

It's best to leave the site on foot to get into Milford on Sea. The village centre is only 10 minutes away and the coast a little further. If the short stroll is enough to get you thirsty then try stopping in The Beach House, a fine pub with great sea views and a child-friendly garden that backs onto the cliffs. A visit to Hurst Castle also offers an excellent walk along the beach and acts as a wonderful lookout point for views of the Solent Coast as well as, on a clear day, the distant Isle of Wight. But from the battlements it's inland that often catches the eye, as the New Forest sweeps away before you, fronted by the rooftops of classic Hampshire villages.

The views from the castle capture the brilliant location of this campsite. With cycle-friendly woodlands to explore, beaches on the doorstep, and more, Muddycreek Farm has a wealth of activities in the vicinity while the site itself has a relaxed feel. When you want to revel in the atmosphere of the outdoors, simply light a campfire, grab a skewer and enjoy toasting marshmallows beneath the stars.

COOL FACTOR A brief but brilliant campsite on a New Forest pony farm.

WHO'S IN Tents, families, couples, small family groups, dogs – yes. Caravans, campervans, motorhomes, groups – no.

ON SITE 60 pitches (6 with electrical hook-ups; so book early if you need power). Showers, toilets and washing-up facilities, plus a freezer for ice packs. Small campfires permitted; wood for sale at reception. Muddycreek breeds New Forest ponies and riding is easily arranged with Burley Manor Riding School – ask onsite for details. It's also possible for kids to enjoy short rides for free, when weather and time permits.

OFF SITE The farm is within walking distance of Milford on Sea, a village well-stocked with shops, pubs and restaurants. From its shingle beach there is a lovely walk along the coast to Barton-on-Sea, skirting the top of a low cliff. Hurst Castle (08703 331181) makes for another great walk. Start at the pretty village of Keyhaven – little more than a cluster of boats with a great pub – and take one of the regular seasonal ferries across to the old fort. Once you've finished exploring and admired the views, you can walk back via the 1½-mile shingle spit, returning to Keyhaven via a narrow road beside a marshy nature reserve.

FOOD & DRINK Milford on Sea is technically a village but its town-size proportions mean it has a good choice of food and drink options. For a traditional pub try The Smugglers Inn (01590 644414) right in the heart of town, or The White Horse (01590 642360) near the village green. The Beach House (01590 643044) is a particularly good spot, too, serving local draft ales and good-quality food inside a fantastic Art Deco building.

GETTING THERE Travel towards Everton on the A337 and turn on to the B3058 signed Milford on Sea. After 1 mile you'll see the main village sign; turn immediately right into the field.

PUBLIC TRANSPORT The nearest train stations are Lymington and New Milton, with bus services to Milford from both.

OPEN Open for 28 days in August only.

THE DAMAGE Adults £8/£16 (weeknight/weekend-night), children (3–14yrs) £4/£8, under-3s free. Dogs free.

Lepe Beach Campsite

Lepe Road, Blackfield, Southampton, Hampshire SO45 1AD   03301 000842   eazycamp.co.uk

There's no doubt the canniest campers come to the Hampshire coast. Those with a stripy windbreak under one arm and a copy of *Lonely Planet* under the other often flock to the South West counties, but this quieter stretch of coastline – and the neighbouring New Forest National Park – is an ideal spot to avoid the crowds. Not only can you stroll along wide beaches and boardwalk your way through marshy nature reserves but, if the British weather takes a turn for the worst, there's the added insurance of the national park's genteel villages, museums and country homes just a stone's throw away.

Only metres from the beach, Lepe Beach Campsite, first opened in 2017, is a traditional camping field that offers nothing flashy but instead focuses on doing the basics well. Very well, in fact. Facilities are immaculately kept, pitches are flat and well maintained and campfires are permitted, with firepits available to hire and wood for purchase. Campervans and caravans are not allowed, giving the whole campsite a peaceful, informal ambience – you can pitch where you like, with enough space that you needn't tread on others' toes – and if you really can't bear roughing it, there are pre-furnished tents which include camp beds, camping chairs and plenty of cooking utensils.

Despite hardly advertising, the campsite's first summer got off to an extremely popular start and prompted a wealth of additional investment for the following years. Toilet facilities and drainage have been drastically improved and a gravel entrance and exit stops the place from becoming muddy. They're all small changes but show the owner's attention to detail and willingness to improve what is, in essence, still a beautifully paired-back and simple camping experience.

In keeping with this, the campsite doesn't have a playground of its own, but it backs onto Lepe Country Park where there's a large picnic area, climbing frame and swings for littl'uns to fly around on. Really, the country park and the campsite seem to roll into one, making it a thoroughly family-friendly location, with the added bonus of Lepe Beach Café and Shop down on the waterfront, which serves afternoon tea and delicious homemade cakes.

The views from Lepe Beach Campsite's enviable vantage point are ridiculously picturesque. Ferries crawl across the water towards the Isle of Wight, which covers much of the distant horizon and, to the west, the marsh and sand flats of the Solent National Nature Reserve unfurl. If you do venture inland, the charming villages of Beaulieu and Exbury Gardens are less than 15 minutes by car, although the New Forest is such a paradise for walkers, horseriders and cyclists that you could just as easily forget about the car altogether.

COOL FACTOR Instant beach access out front and the New Forest National Park just behind, plus fantastic views across the Solent.

WHO'S IN Tents – yes. Caravans, campervans, twin-axle vehicles, large single-sex groups, dogs – no.

ON SITE Up to 100 flat grass camping pitches and 25 pre-pitched, ready-furnished tents. Toilets, showers, washing-up area, general and recycling bins, ice-pack hire, ice-pack re-freezing (50p per pack), firewood packs and firepit hire (£3 per night; minimum 2 nights). Beach fishing available. Pre-erected tents include camp beds, camping chairs, cutlery, crockery, cooking utensils, small chopping board, cooking table, washing-up bowl and a gas cooking stove – see website for further details.

OFF SITE Just the other side of the hedge/fence, Lepe Country Park has a children's play area and there is a picnic space with tables – a nice spot to enjoy the view if you're lunching at the campsite. It's a 150-yard stroll down to sandy Lepe Beach while, 100 yards in the opposite direction, there is also a nature reserve. Venture inland to Exbury Gardens (023 8089 1203), where there are expansive woodlands and abundant rhododendrons and azaleas, plus steam-train rides in high season. A little further afield lies the renowned ship-building village of Bucklers Hard, now a popular tourist stop. It's 7 miles to Beaulieu, home to the National Motor Museum (01590 612345) but also a lovely village to explore in its own right.

Families can also take refuge in Paultons Park (023 8081 4442) – a theme park (home to Peppa Pig World) around 25 minute's drive away.

FOOD & DRINK It's 2 miles to Langley where there is a small supermarket, pubs, takeaway food and a cash-point (only cash is accepted for most things at the campsite). For a daytime treat, drive the 3 miles to Exbury Gardens (023 8089 1203) where Mr Eddie's Tea Rooms (023 8089 8737) offers tasty cakes and treats. The Montagu Arms in Beaulieu (01590 612324) serves good pub food and also high-end fare in its excellent Terrace restaurant.

GETTING THERE From Southampton follow the A362 south, continue as it becomes the Hythe bypass and then the A362 again. After a while you will begin to see brown tourist signs for Lepe Country Park. Where the A362 ends, at a roundabout on the edge of Holbury, take the second exit and continue on this road for a further 3 miles. The campsite is next to the Lepe Country Park car park.

PUBLIC TRANSPORT During the school holidays there is a direct, hourly Beach Bus service to Lepe Beach from Beaulieu and Lymington.

OPEN Whitsun May half-term–end of August.

THE DAMAGE A grass pitch and up to 4 people from £32.50 (2-night minimum); extra campers £2.50. Pre-pitched tents and up to 4 people from £57; extra campers £11. Saturday and Wednesday start days only.

Grange Farm

Brighstone Bay, Grange Chine, Isle of Wight PO30 4DA   01983 740296   grangefarmholidays.com

The ultra-green, festival-hosting Isle of Wight has reinvented itself as a hip little island offering something for everyone, with exceptional waves for surfers, as well as kite-surfing, paragliding, and summer events that attract new crowds every year. The isle is shaped a bit like a front-on cow's head with, at its temple, fittingly, a town called Cowes. At its respective ears sit the towns of Yarmouth and Ryde, both of which have regular ferry services to the mainland. And perched atop tall cliffs, behind the beach at Brighstone (about midway down the left of the cow's jawline), sits the utterly charming Grange Farm.

It's a lovely, unspoiled site situated in a beautiful part of the island. Two flat, grassy fields go right to the edge of the cliff and there's an overflow field across the road, aptly christened the 'Cool Camping' Field. You'll need a sturdy tent for the winds blowing across the top of these fields, but the reward is a panoramic view across the sea and an easy scramble down to the beach below. It's also a family-run, family-friendly site that is left deliberately undeveloped. Kids will love getting close to its Noah's Ark of farm animals, including llamas (Delboy and Rodney), kunekune pigs, goats, water buffalo and a variety of poultry. Plus there is a play area for ball games and a children's playground, with boats and trains, stepping stones and rope bridges, in case the beach should lose its appeal – though parents should be mindful of the cliff edge at all times. All in all, a friendly and wonderfully varied site in a marvellous location on this multi-faceted isle.

COOL FACTOR Clifftop pitches with panoramic sea views and easy access to action and adventure.

WHO'S IN Tents, campervans, caravans, dogs (in caravans) – yes. Groups – sometimes, by arrangement.

ON SITE Two fields with 60 pitches, most with electrical hook-ups; extra tent field only open for 28 days in July/August and 5 pods for glamping. A heated block has 15 showers, a coin-operated bath, toilets, and washing-up sinks. Laundry, hairdryers, phone and drinks machine. Campfires allowed on the beach below. Onsite barn conversions and static caravans also available.

OFF SITE Head out surfing/paragliding/kite-surfing, or take it easy exploring nearby Newport, whose Roman remains can be supplemented by the Roman villa at Brading (01983 406223), which has a visitor centre and museum. Cowes is also one of the isle's liveliest towns. Treat yourself to a visual extravaganza of water, beach, urban, air and land sports at the annual White Air Extreme Sports Festival (late September or early October).

FOOD & DRINK The Blacksmiths Arms (01983 529263), a little way inland near Newport, serves food and has a pleasant beer garden. Check out the local plonk at Adgestone Vineyard (01983 402503) in Sandown, one of the oldest vineyards in the UK, half a mile from the Roman villa at Brading. The Three Bishops in Brighstone (01983 740226; a ¾-mile stroll) is a decent family-friendly pub and has a pool table and open fire.

GETTING THERE From Fishbourne/Cowes follow the signs to Newport then Carisbrooke. At Carisbrooke take the A3323 to Shorwell and Brighstone. Just before Brighstone, turn left by the church and follow New Road all the way to the end. Grange Farm is opposite. From Yarmouth, follow the signs to Freshwater Bay, then the A3055 for 5 miles, looking out for Grange Farm on the right.

PUBLIC TRANSPORT From Yarmouth/Newport, take bus 7 to Brighstone. Get off at the Three Bishops and walk to the site.

OPEN March–November.

THE DAMAGE Pitch and 2 people £19–£34.50, electric pitches £22–£36.50. Extra adults £4–£4.50, children (4–13yrs) £2.50–£3, under-4s free. Dog £2. Pods £32–£51.50.

Whitecliff Bay

Whitecliff Bay Holiday Park, Hillway Road, Bembridge, Isle of Wight PO35 5PL   01983 872671   wight-holidays.com

Only a few miles off the Hampshire coast, the Isle of Wight does it's best to bottle the classic British holiday. An ever-popular retreat for walkers, cyclists and the bucket-and-spade brigade since Queen Victoria's reign, the island's leading appeal is its countless outdoor activities, mild climate and dense green hills that roll down to over 20 miles of unspoiled beaches. Not only that, the last decade has seen a more contemporary ingredient added to its towns and villages, attracting a new generation of campers, with fancy gastropubs, vintage antique shops and huge international music festivals.

Situated on the island's picturesque east coast, Whitecliff Bay is a great spot for families and small groups. The site offers a wide range of accommodation, with over 400 pitches for traditional campers set on a south-facing gentle slope with stunning countryside views, along with a variety of glamping options in the 'Canvas Village', where a dozen bell tents and 'Canvas Cottages' are ideal for those who don't want to compromise on comfort.

If you're a camper striving for solitude then Whitecliff Bay probably isn't going to be for you. But what the park lacks in intimacy, it makes up for in facilities, with large outdoor and indoor-heated pools, a secluded sandy beach (with café), two restaurants and a supermarket that sells all the essentials.

The Isle of Wight measures only 23 miles by 13 miles, and much of it is designated an 'Area of Outstanding Natural Beauty'. The east coast is lined with charming Victorian resorts (such as nearby Sandown), while the scenic west coast is less developed and home to the pretty port of Yarmouth and the Needles, pinnacles of chalk towering out of the sea. Perfect walking territory, the island is criss-crossed with 500 miles of footpaths. If you don't feel like tackling the 64-mile coastal path, then try the Tennyson Trail. Named after former Poet Laureate Alfred Lord Tennyson, this picturesque walk starts at Carisbrooke Castle and continues over Brighstone Down towards Alum Bay. Keep your eyes peeled for the 'barrows' on Mottistone Down, a burial site that dates back 4000 years.

Days certainly fly by on the Isle of Wight. Whichever way you turn, you'll find spectacular views, a plethora of attractions and miles of untouched coastline. Back at Whitecliff Bay the evenings bring the good times too. Don't worry campers, no jazz hands here; the onsite entertainment includes artists from the West End and, in the summer months, there are even outdoor film screenings overlooking the beautiful twilight silhouettes of the bay. But if the 'holiday park' feel isn't to your taste, well, just kick back, light up the BBQ and take in those expansive countryside views.

COOL FACTOR Heaps of facilities, yards from the sea.

WHO'S IN Tents, campervans, caravans, families, groups and dogs (max 2 per pitch) – yes. Hen and stag parties – no.

ON SITE Plenty of spaces for regular camping, plus 20 bell tents for glampers. 2 shower blocks and laundry facilities. Small shop (open during peak times), bar (with free Wi-Fi). Indoor and outdoor heated pools, club house, indoor soft playground, outdoor playground and sports lounge. Daytime activities include archery, axe-throwing, paintball, crossbow, 'footgolf', snorkelling and more.

OFF SITE The English Heritage property Osborne House (01983 200022) – built in the 19th century for Queen Victoria and Prince Albert – offers the chance to visit a royal seaside palace in the style of an Italian Renaissance *palazzo*, while 12th-century Carisbrooke Castle (01983 523112) is best known as the place where King Charles I was imprisoned: walk the castle walls or play bowls on the green. Kids will love dressing up as Norman soldiers and meeting the castle's famous donkeys, while grown-ups can take a stroll around the new Edwardian-style Princess Beatrice Garden.

FOOD & DRINK Onsite options include the Nab Bar & Restaurant, which serves food throughout the day, Tuppeny Café, offering homemade food and postcard views, or The Culver Diner for fast food. Away from Whitecliff, The Culver Downs Café provides simple homemade goodies in a spectacular location and the dog-friendly Crab & Lobster Inn (01983 872244) overlooks beautiful Bembridge Ledge.

GETTING THERE Following the A3055 Ryde–Sandown road, take the Marshcombe Shute south-east turn off to Bembridge by The Yarbridge Inn. Turn left on to the B3395 Sandown Road and follow this to Bembridge. Passing Bembridge Airport on the left, take a right after the Propeller Inn and then the first left on to Hilway Road. Whitecliff is ¼ mile along on the right.

PUBLIC TRANSPORT The Southern Vectis 8 bus runs via Ryde and Brading railway stations to the campsite entrance.

OPEN March–November.

THE DAMAGE Standard pitches £4–£25, serviced and 'super' pitches up to £47; all include 6 people.

Shear Barn Holidays

Barley Lane, Hastings, East Sussex TN35 5DX   01424 423583   shearbarn.com

Situated high above the East Sussex coast, Shear Barn offers no-fuss camping and easy access to beaches, historic Hastings Old Town and wonderful walks through the Hastings Country Park Nature Reserve.

This campsite has everything you need for a comfortable stay, with clean, modern shower blocks, level pitches and plenty of space. It's family friendly, with a children's play park, launderette and a small shop selling essentials in the reception area. Guests are also welcome to use the facilities on site, including an indoor swimming pool and a well-appointed bar that serves reasonably priced food all day and boasts spectacular views over the rolling countryside down to the English Channel.

A 25-minute stroll through the park (via the funicular railway) lies picturesque Hastings Old Town which, thanks to its artsy community, has no shortage of cafés, restaurants and independent shops selling everything from antiques to artisan bread. On the seafront you'll find The Stade where the tall black net huts of the town's still-working fishing fleet stand alongside the Jerwood Gallery of modern art. The park also gives direct access to various cycle paths and walks, both down to the coast and the town through woodland and rolling green countryside.

This stretch of the East Sussex coast runs for miles offering a mix of sand, shingle and pebble beaches. Camber Sands is a classic bucket 'n' spade sandy beach, bordered by dunes and popular with the kite-surfing fraternity. Winchelsea is much quieter thanks to the shingle beach at high tide. But, with the iconic groynes framing the landscape,

it is just as picturesque. Fairlight Glen Beach is a lovely secluded spot beneath the Hastings Country Park, with shingle, low-tide sand and rounded rocks to explore.

This is, of course, 1066 country and there's heaps of history to be discovered. England's most famous battle didn't actually take place in Hastings at all but six miles away in what is now the town of Battle. William the Conquerer erected the magnificent Battle Abbey on the spot where King Harold fell and although the original church was destroyed during Henry VIII's reign, the ruins can still be explored. The battlefield visitor centre also gives you heaps of information and an opportunity to learn more about this iconic historical site, with interactive exhibitions and audio tours available for both the battleground and the abbey.

COOL FACTOR Perfectly placed for exploring historic Hastings and the south coast.

WHO'S IN Tents, caravans, motorhomes, dogs, groups – yes.

ON SITE Clean wash-blocks with showers, toilets, washbasins, hairdryers and shaving points, babychanging facilities, washing-up areas, children's play area and family BBQ area. There is a small shop selling essentials and papers. Wi-Fi, laundry and use of the indoor swimming pool are available at an extra charge.

OFF SITE Hastings Old Town is a 25-minute walk away and home to the Jerwood Gallery of modern art (01424 425809) and the award-winning Shipwreck Museum (01424 437452). Blue Reef Aquarium (0844 5499088) offers visitors an underwater safari with turtles, sharks, rays and octopuses. Soak up the history of the Battle of Hastings by visiting the English Heritage-run Abbey and Battlefield (01424 775705), where audio tours and CGI film bring this brutal battle back to life. Further inland, Bodiam Castle (01580 830196) is a fairytale fortress with spiral staircases and imposing battlements to explore. The popular beach of Camber Sands is favoured by bathers and kite-surfers alike.

FOOD & DRINK There's no shortage of mouth-watering places to eat in Hastings Old Town – The Two Bulls Steakhouse (01424 640258) serves top-notch steak cooked over a charcoal BBQ, Maggie's (01424 430205) serves what is frequently crowned the best fish and chips in Britain, and The Little Larder café (01424 424364) offers lighter bites and coffees. Independent eateries abound, though, so it's always worth taking a stroll to see if you stumble upon a hidden gem.

GETTING THERE From Hastings, leave the A259 by All Saint's Church on to Harold Road (both road and church are on your right-hand side). Follow Harold Road for ¼ mile then turn right on to Barley Lane and follow for ½ mile to the campsite (on your right).

PUBLIC TRANSPORT Hastings train station is a bit of a walk from the site but nearby Ore station is a half an hour's walk or a 10-minute cycle ride away.

OPEN March–October.

THE DAMAGE From £16 per tent per night.

Cliff House

Minsmere Road, Dunwich, Saxmundham, Suffolk IP17 3DQ   01728 648282   cliffhouseholidays.co.uk

If you look at the website before your visit, don't be put off by the emphasis on holiday cottages and caravans. This 30-acre woodland site has lots of prime tent pitches among the trees and on the lawn in front of the house. If hide-and-seeking in the woods, peddling the path through the site or ball games aren't enough to keep the kids busy, they can always head off to the playground for climbing, swinging and sliding, or to the indoor family games room for table football and pool. Or go and visit the neighbours – the National Trust's Dunwich Heath Coastal Centre and Beach is right next door.

Steps take you down to the stony band of beach itself, at the bottom of the cliff, where you can fly kites, beachcomb or paddle in the sea, or take the short walk to the nearby Coastal Centre, for porpoise and seal spotting in the Seawatch Room. The RSPB's Minsmere nature reserve is also on your doorstep and home to fantastic nature trails and birdwatching opportunities in both woodland and wetland, beach and dunes. You can join birdwatching safaris and the birding hides are open for anyone to use.

The combination of quiet woodland camping, days on the beach and a wealth of natural treasures to explore make for an all-round gem of a campsite. The site is also constantly modernising, with an onsite bar, electricity on almost every pitch and a second, newly refurbished shower block, but thankfully it hasn't ruined the small-scale feel – one in which you can pedal your bike safely around by day and snooze peacefully beneath the trees at night.

COOL FACTOR Woodland pitches with direct access to the beach, plus a great playground for the kids.

WHO'S IN Tents, campervans, caravans, dogs, groups... the lot!

ON SITE 120 pitches (50 for tents) spread throughout the woods or on the flat grassy lawn in front of the house. Two shower blocks with showers, toilets and washbasins, plus washing-up sinks and a launderette with 2 washing machines and 2 tumble-dryers. Outside playground and indoor games room, plus a pub, restaurant and small shop (selling all the basics). Immediate step-access to the beach.

OFF SITE The National Trust's Dunwich Heath Coastal Centre and Beach (01728 648501) is nextdoor to the site, as is the RSPB's Minsmere nature reserve (01728 648281) with hides and nature trails. A 10-minute drive (or hour's stroll) takes you to Walberswick. Here you can do a spot of crabbing (it's the home of the British Open Crabbing Championships) before hopping on to a foot ferry for a short ride over the water to Southwold Harbour, from where Southwold itself, with its sandy beach, colourful bathing huts and quirky pier, is a 10-minute walk away.

FOOD & DRINK The onsite pub – The 12 Lost Churches – does traditional grub and children's meals, and the National Trust tea room along the beach at the old Coastguard Cottages (01728 648501) has splendid views and serves some of the best puds on the Suffolk coast.

GETTING THERE Head north from Ipswich and leave the A12 (right) at the sign for Westleton and Dunwich. Carry on to the end of the road and, at Westleton, turn left. Drive through the village and turn right at the top of the hill towards Dunwich. Continue until you see brown caravan signs and turn right on to Minsmere Road. The campsite is 1 mile down on the left.

OPEN All year.

THE DAMAGE Pitch and 2 people £15–£35. Adults free–£5.50; children (4–14yrs) free–£3.20. Dogs free–£1.50.

Manor Farm

East Runton, Cromer, Norfolk NR27 9PR   01263 512858   manorfarmcampsite.co.uk

Your arrival at Manor Farm is just the thing for creating the right atmosphere. As you pootle along between the cobbled and flint barns, with high hedgerows brushing your car on both sides, the site jumps into view. The camping fields are at the top of the hill, with the seaside town of Cromer a mere 10 minutes' walk away. And in the distance, like an ironed-out pancake, you'll see the open blue of the sea.

It's a good view, and this feels like a suitably remote spot to pitch your tent, even though you can walk so easily into town. The fact that you reach the campsite via the farm track and there are no roads nearby means you can let the kids run wild without worrying about traffic thundering past.

And boy do they have the space to roam around here – this site is seriously sprawling. And while it's pretty, the pace is far from being twee, so avoids the blazer-clad crowds of 'Chelsea-on-Sea' at nearby Burnham Market. Instead, you can stroll through charmingly old-fashioned East Runton village at the bottom of the campsite's slope, and on to the local beach – a pebbly affair with excellent rock pools full of glistening sea shells and tiny scuttling crabs.

Manor Farm is a family-owned working farm, so there are lambs and calves to see if you happen to be visiting at Easter, and ponies to pet all year round. The place feels wild and yet you have all the advantages of a small seaside town on your doorstep. It's an ideal combination. And, surveyed over a fresh cuppa from the onsite Cabin Café, there are few spots around here we would rather pitch our tent.

COOL FACTOR Rolling fields with the sea on the horizon and a delightful seaside town within walking distance.

WHO'S IN Tents, campervans, caravans, dogs, groups – yes.

ON SITE 250 standard and serviced pitches, spread across 18 acres. The site feels sprawling but the facilities are never too far away, with 2 shower blocks in each field. There are also 2 laundry rooms with coin-operated washing machines and dryers. Freezers for ice-blocks. Bikes available to hire.

OFF SITE East Runton is a sweet, old-fashioned village, with a butcher, tea room, fish-and-chip shop, even an excellent army surplus store and a hairdresser, so all essentials are covered if you are suddenly struck with a desire to get a perm. You can walk through the campsite into the village, with its pretty green, swings and slides, to East Runton's beach – a quiet spot with good rock pools and nice views to Cromer pier. Cromer and Sheringham are the main local beaches. A short drive away, the National Trust's Fellbrigg Hall (01263 837444) and Sheringham Park (01263 820550) are well worth a visit.

FOOD & DRINK Owned by television chef Galton Blackiston, No1 (01263 515983) is generally considered to be the best fish-and-chip shop in Cromer and also has great sea views from the upstairs dining room. The Pepperpot Restaurant (01263 837578) in West Runton is fantastic, too, but a little more expensive. For local meat try Icarus Hines' butcher (01263 514541) in Cromer or the farm shop at Groveland Farm in Roughton (01263 833777).

GETTING THERE Leave the A149 at the clear brown and white tourist sign that says 'Manor Farm'. Follow the road just into the village and the campsite is on the right.

PUBLIC TRANSPORT There are regular trains to Cromer from Norwich, from where it's a 10-minute walk to the site.

OPEN March–end of October.

THE DAMAGE A pitch and family of 4 from £17.50–£27. Adults £5, children (4–15yrs) £1, under-4s free. Dogs £1.

Scaldbeck Cottage

Stiffkey Road, Morston, Holt, Norfolk NR25 7BJ   01263 740188   bluejacketworkshop.co.uk

Travel along the main north Norfolk coast road between Sheringham and Hunstanton and, just west of the village of Morston, you'll pass a very missable hand-painted sign bearing the legend 'B&B and campsite'. This is Scaldbeck Cottage, which turns out to be a fine-looking traditional Norfolk flint cottage with a small camping field just beyond its garden. It's a thoroughly informal affair and perhaps one of the best campsites anywhere in the whole of Norfolk, let alone the north Norfolk coast.

Access to the site is around the back of the cottage, under some trees and past upturned rowing boats, while a path off through the garden leads to the loo and shower. Do pop a mallet in with your luggage, because although the grass looks soft enough, the ground beneath it is really quite hard after the first inch and will take a certain delight in bending your pegs should you attempt to ram them in with your foot.

Just a five-minute stroll from National Trust-owned Morston Quay, a vast mashy tract of land where boats bob in and out at high tide, the site is ideal for hikers who want a base from which to walk sections of the Norfolk Coast Path. Simply take the excellent Coasthopper bus to whichever point you want to walk along, then hop out to explore the flat, well marked route. To fuel you up, there's a cooked breakfast available (£8) if booked the night before – either a Full English with a slew of homemade ingredients, or a veggie alternative. In the event of fire, famine, pestilence or the sword, the cottage also has a couple of rooms available for B&B.

COOL FACTOR Traditional small-scale camping with seal trips and boating from the old quay just a stroll away.

WHO'S IN Tents, dogs – yes. Campervans, caravans – no.

ON SITE Maximum occupancy of 12 people. A loo, 1 shower, an outdoor washing-up area, picnic tables and recycling bins. Campfires permitted in designated area (must bring your own wood). BBQ and breeze blocks available. No electrical hook-ups.

OFF SITE The 47-mile-long Norfolk Coast Path goes right past the campsite and takes in some of the best bits of the county's coastline, from salt marshes and mudflats to cliffs. Head to Morston Quay (¼ mile away) for seal-watching boat trips with Bean's Boats (01263 740038) or Temple Boats (01263 740791), which take you out to Blakeney Point. The campsite owners are happy to book it for you. There is also a sailing school (01263 740704) at Morston Quay with various courses for children and adults.

FOOD & DRINK Grab a light bite at the Wiveton Hall Café (01263 740515), famous for its appearance on the BBC cult reality show Normal For Norfolk – the food is excellent and you'll also be contributing to keeping the stately pile alive. For a good pub, try The Anchor Inn (01263 741392), a short walk away in Morston along the coast path – the food is excellent so booking ahead is essential. The Wiveton Bell (01263 740101), a couple of miles inland on the other side of Blakeney, also serves great food and has a lovely garden.

GETTING THERE The campsite is just off the A149 coast road just west of Morston. Look for signs to the Bluejacket Workshop and small handmade signs at the site entrance.

PUBLIC TRANSPORT Take a train to Sheringham, the nearest train station (11 miles away), and then hop on the Coasthopper bus, which stops right outside the site.

OPEN March–October (or later, if weather permits).

THE DAMAGE £6 per person per night.

Deepdale Backpackers

Deepdale Farm, Burnham Deepdale, Norfolk, PE31 8DD   01485 210256   deepdalebackpackers.co.uk

Come mid September, most people of sound mind put any thoughts of camping to rest. It's not just because the days start to turn colder but because there aren't that many campsites that stay open once the leaves begin to curl and drop. Nudging the north Norfolk coastline, Deepdale Farm in Burnham Deepdale is a rare exception.

Some believe there is no better time to visit Norfolk than autumn – the hedgerows are pregnant with blackberries and the county is a vision of russet-coloured forests and blush-coloured clouds. And with original owner Jason Borthwick now back in charge of the local farm campsite, Deepdale's 80 pitches are once again the ideal base for exploring the delights of north Norfolk, whatever the season.

Backing on to open fields that run away towards a brow of trees and nearby Barrow Common, Deepdale Farm is a long-established spot that has featured in *Cool Camping* guidebooks since the early days. It's always hosted an enthusiastic programme of events, with everything from organised stargazing to cookery classes with local produce. But in any case there are diversions a-plenty in and around Burnham Deepdale. Kick-start the morning with a coffee at the café nextdoor, and stock up on necessities at the nearby supermarket or onsite camping shop before hiring a bike or pulling on your walking boots. You're so near to the coast here that an excursion to the water's edge is a must – stroll to Brancanster Staithe to watch the bobbing dinghies and buy the freshest of fresh crab from the shack.

COOL FACTOR Established excellence beside the coast path.

WHO'S IN Tents, small campervans, dogs – yes. Caravans, big groups, young groups – no.

ON SITE 80 grass camping pitches, 22 eco-friendly cubicles with showers, loos and sinks, 2 male toilets and 2 urinals, 3 female toilets, a unisex toilet block plus washing-up facilities. The water is heated by solar panels, with gas boiler back-up. Along with an onsite camping shop, the excellent Deepdale Café next door serves everything from cooked breakfasts and burgers to homemade soups and sweet treats.

OFF SITE Follow the coast path west to Brancaster Staithe harbour, where you can revel in the muddy marshes and go crabbing off the old wharf. Or escape to the posh boutiques of Burnham Market – it's not called Chelsea-on-Sea for nothing. Further afield, there's the huge, pine-backed expanse of sand at Holkham Bay, and the honest seaside town of Wells-next-the-Sea just beyond.

FOOD & DRINK The Deepdale Café next door serves everything from quality English breakfasts to wholesome homemade soups (including evening meals in summer). The White Horse (01485 210262), a 5-minute walk away, is a buzzy gastropub serving local fish and shellfish, including cockles, mussels and oysters from the beds at the bottom of the garden.

GETTING THERE The campsite is just off the A149 coast road, about midway between Hunstanton and Wells-next-the-Sea. Look out for Deepdale Market and the site is right beside it.

PUBLIC TRANSPORT Take the Coasthopper bus from Kings Lynn to Burnham Deepdale and you'll alight right by the site.

OPEN All year.

THE DAMAGE Pitches from £6 plus £1 per person (low season); £12 plus £2 per person (mid season), £18 plus £3 per person (high season).

Wold Farm

Bempton Lane, Flamborough, Bridlington, East Yorkshire YO15 1AT   01262 850536   woldfarmcampsite.co.uk

Opened on the Yorkshire coast back in 2008, this is a site for lovers of open fields and big skies. Three-quarters of a mile up a rough track, Wold Farmhouse stands in wondrous isolation on the great chalk promontory that is Flamborough Head. There are several individual camping fields, each enjoying uninterrupted views over the sheep-filled meadows to both Flamborough lighthouses (new one on the left, old one on the right), with a sliver of sea to top it off. There's a new toilet and shower block with pot-washing facilities.

This site is an Eldorado for walkers, birdwatchers and beach-lovers alike. Take the campsite's private footpath to the cliffs, just a 5-minute walk away, and you can see puffins, gannets, skuas and countless other birds, or do the circular nine-mile walk of the entire headland, taking in no fewer than five spectacular Yorkshire coast beaches and bays along the way. Meanwhile, those who enjoy the odd tipple will be encouraged to learn that, despite its apparently remote location, there are no fewer than nine drinking establishments within a mile and a half of the campsite.

There are also so many things to do in this corner of Yorkshire, with Bridlington, Filey and Scarborough only a short drive away, that the owners present campers with a welcome pack. It includes information on Sewerby Hall, Zoo and Gardens, three miles away, which in 2009 successfully defended its title as Britain's Best Picnic Spot. Why not take along a sandwich and a flask and find out what all the fuss is about?

COOL FACTOR A clifftop, Yorkshire paradise for bird-lovers, beach bums and walkers.

WHO'S IN Tents, campervans, caravans – yes.

ON SITE 2 fairly flat fields with 48 spacious grass pitches, some with electrical hook-ups, alongside glamping pods and bell tents for hire. New toilet and shower block with drinking water and washing-up facilities. A private scenic path leads to the cliffs. Quiet picnic area.

OFF SITE The Georgian country house and 50-acre estate at Sewerby Hall, Zoo and Gardens (01262 673769) is a lovely spot for those with an interest in animals and/or history. The former will enjoy the RSPB reserve at Bempton Cliffs too. You should also consider taking the Puffin cruise (01262 850959), which leaves from North Pier in Bridlington 5 miles away, on which you can spot puffins from late May to mid July and skuas in September; advance booking is advised. Flamborough Head Lighthouse (01262 673769), 3 miles from Wold Farm campsite, was built in 1806 and offers superb views.

FOOD & DRINK There's a pub for every taste in Flamborough, and a surprising number of them given its seemingly remote location, but the one with the best reputation for food is The Seabirds (01262 850242) on Tower Street.

GETTING THERE Take the Scarborough road out of Bridlington and turn left on to Marton Road – the B1255. Follow this for a couple of miles, past Bridlington Bay golf course, to Flamborough, through the village and beyond.

PUBLIC TRANSPORT There are train stations at Bridlington and Bempton; the 510 bus from Bridlington runs to Flamborough.

OPEN Late March–November.

THE DAMAGE Pitch and 2 people £14–£16 per night; extra adults £5, children £3. Electric £4. Bank Holiday surcharge £5. Glamping pods £40–£45 a night.

Crows Nest

Crows Nest Caravan Park, Gristhorpe, Filey, North Yorkshire YO14 9PS   01723 582206   crowsnestcaravanpark.com

Crows Nest is a tale of two campsites. The first is a large holiday park with a bar, café, fish-and-chip shop, indoor swimming pool and row upon row of static caravans. Not exactly *Cool Camping*. But venture a little further and, in sharp contrast, you'll find a large tents-only field with panoramic views over the sea and across the Yorkshire Wolds and Vale of Pickering. A children's playground forms a handy boundary between the two very different areas.

The tent field climbs up and then slopes gently down towards the clifftop. There's room for around 200 tents (and the odd campervan) on a pitch-where-you-like basis. As you head up the hill, you'll spy some secluded areas surrounded by hedges for small groups of tents, and the closer you get to the sea, the quieter and more peaceful the campsite seems to become. Large family groups head for the serviced pitches near the playground – a huge kiddy paradise with different climbing frames and slides for different-sized children – while a mixture of couples, groups and families spread across the rest of the space.

From the camping meadow there is a small path that connects up with the clifftop Cleveland Way footpath and the adventurous and sure of foot can also scramble down a narrow cliff trail to the shingle beach at Gristhorpe Bay below. If you're lucky, you might spot members of the local seal colony that live on and around the rocks here. If you can't spot them in windy weather then it's still worth the trip. The cacophony of the waves is an attraction itself.

COOL FACTOR Breathtaking views and all the facilities of a holiday park but with a traditional tents-only feel.

WHO'S IN Tents, campervans, caravans, dogs, groups – yes.

ON SITE The large tent field accepts around 150 tents without electrical hook-ups. There are also 20 tent pitches with electric hook-ups (near the play area), plus 50 touring caravan pitches and 220 static caravans in a separate area. An award-winning ablutions block sits on the edge of the camping field, featuring ladies and gents facilities, family shower rooms, a disabled shower room, pot-wash and laundry. There's a well-stocked shop along with other facilities in the main holiday-park.

OFF SITE The Cleveland Way runs along the clifftop in front of the site and takes you into Filey (2 miles) in one direction, and Scarborough (5 miles) in the other. The former has an excellent volunteer-run museum (01723 515013) in an old fisherman's cottage (great for rainy days), while the latter boasts 2 bays, 2 beaches and a fantastic 12th-century castle on the headland inbetween. Take the Victorian funicular train to the south bay and harbour, while Scarborough's SEA LIFE Sanctuary (01723 373414) and the Peasholm Park Japanese gardens are behind North Bay.

FOOD & DRINK The restaurant at the Copper Horse (01723 862029) in Seamer has a theatrical theme and serves award-winning food. For great fish and chips there is a takeaway onsite or you should head to Inghams (01723 513320) on Belle Vue Street in Filey.

GETTING THERE The site is just off the A165 between Scarborough and Filey. A couple of miles north of Filey there's a roundabout with a Jet petrol station on the corner. Turn left here and Crows Nest is the second caravan park on the left.

PUBLIC TRANSPORT Bus 120 runs between Scarborough, Filey and Bridlington and Crows Nest has its very own stop.

OPEN March–October.

THE DAMAGE Tent (and up to 4 people) £25–£40 per night.

Hooks House Farm

Whitby Road, Robin Hood's Bay, North Yorkshire YO22 4PE   01947 880283   hookshousefarm.co.uk

Robin Hood's Bay, near Whitby in North Yorkshire, is an area steeped in romance and intrigue. Its very name is a mystery: there's nothing to link this place with the infamous green-clad hero of Sherwood Forest, but nonetheless the name hints at a legendary past. What's certain is that this was smuggler country, and arriving at Hooks House Farm late on a clear evening under a full moon, it's not hard to picture the scenes from long ago, with the breathtaking sight of the wide sweep of the bay laid out beneath you in the silvery moonlight as shadowy figures emerged from small wooden boats and scuttled towards the shore clutching their loot.

Throughout the 18th century, locals crippled by high taxes turned to illegal imports to make money, receiving tobacco, brandy, rum and silk from Europe. Gangs of smugglers used a network of underground passages and secret tunnels to deliver the stash inland, making a tidy profit in the process. Even now, the charming town of Robin Hood's Bay has the smugglers' feel, with unfeasibly narrow streets and tight passageways – although these days you're more likely to stumble across a second-hand bookshop than hidden contraband. Ancient fishermen's cottages cling to the near-vertical slope as the cliff drops down to a little harbour at the water's edge. In addition to this older part of town there's a newer, Victorian enclave on the flat ground at the top, where the well-ordered mansions are a world apart from the cobbled jumble below. The volunteer-run museum, reached via the narrow cobbled pathways and steps, sheds some light on the town's past, with a model of a smuggler's house along with stories of shipwrecks and historic rescues.

Although the bay is picturesque, it doesn't have a beach to tempt sunbathers. The ground is dark and rocky – more suitable for bracing walks, rockpool explorations, and fossil-hunting than lazing around – and at the friendly, family-run campsite at Hooks House Farm, high up on the hill above town, you couldn't wish for a better vantage point; from its grassy field sloping gently down towards the sea you can watch the tide wash in and out over the whole sweep of shoreline, or gaze across a colourful patchwork of sheep- and cow-dotted fields, woods, rolling hills and moors.

If you're feeling energetic, the surrounding countryside (including the Yorkshire Moors National Park) is perfectly placed for outdoor fun. The disused railway line that runs through here on its way from Scarborough to Whitby has been transformed into a popular walking and cycling path, and forms part of the long-distance Moor-to-Sea path. Robin Hood's Bay also marks the eastern end of the classic Coast-to-Coast Walk, while the Cleveland Way, a 110-mile National Trail between Helmsley and Filey, also follows the coast here. If you're after shorter walks, try the half-mile stretch from the campsite down to the town, where you'll find several cosy pubs – all great venues for discussing smuggling, fossil-hunting and speculating on how Robin Hood's Bay got its intriguing name.

COOL FACTOR Panoramic views over the sea and the North York Moors from peaceful, low-key meadows.

WHO'S IN Tents, campervans, caravans, dogs – yes. Groups and noisy folk – no.

ON SITE Pitches for 50 tents and 20 campervans/caravans spread out across a gently sloping field. A second field originally used for camping is now left solely as a family play area. Clean but basic facilities, with 3 showers, 5 basins, and 4 toilets in separate blocks for men and women; there's also a block with private cubicles. A further block has 3 washing-up sinks, a kettle, a microwave, fridge and freezers; and there's recycling for paper, cardboard, plastic tins, cans and glass. The campsite is next to a road, but it's not inundated with vehicles and you're more likely to be bothered by the cries of seagulls and bleatings of sheep than by traffic noise. No campfires.

OFF SITE Robin Hood's Bay's narrow streets are fun to explore and the town has its own cinema at the Swell Café Bar (01947 880180). With original 1820s seating, it feels more like a theatre than a cinema. Whitby is only 6 miles up the coast and its abbey (01947 603568) is a good place to start your visit to the town. Take in the views over Whitby and the coast (and the tea shop) before you head down the famous 199 steps into the bustling, higgledy-piggledy streets of the old town and harbour. If you're here with kids, the harbour walls make a good spot for crabbing, while the beach awaits for kite-flying, fossil-hunting and exploring rock pools at low tide. Several boat trips leave daily from the harbour, and between mid September and early November the Speksioneer and its sister boat, the Esk Belle II ('The Big Yellow Boat') set off in search of minke whales that follow the shoals of North Sea

herring as they swim down from the Arctic to their spawning grounds off the coast here. If you're lucky, you might also spot porpoises, dolphins and seals and, even if you're not, you'll definitely see some beautiful coastal scenery. The 21-mile ex-Scarborough-to-Whitby train line runs through the upper village and makes a great hiking/biking route – bike rental is available from Trailways at nearby Hawsker (01947 820207).

FOOD & DRINK Pubs in the town include The Dolphin (01947 880337), which has a cosy, old-world feel, and The Bay Hotel (01947 880278), where you can overlook the bay from the quayside as you enjoy a drink or meal. Try also The Laurel Inn (01947 880400), which has a bar carved from solid rock. The Bramblewick restaurant (01947 880187) is a café by day and offers candle-lit dining by night, and kids will love the old-fashioned Browns sweetshop (01947 881288), with its traditional sweets and handmade chocolates. The town also has a good fishmonger's and lovely fresh bread is sold at the General Store. In Whitby, The Magpie Café (01947 602058) is considered one of Britain's best chippies, while fish foodies should also try Green's restaurant (01947 600284).

GETTING THERE Heading south from Whitby on the A171, take the B1447 signposted to Robin Hood's Bay. Hooks House Farm is on the right, ½ mile before the village.

PUBLIC TRANSPORT Arriva buses from Scarborough to Middlesbrough run through Robin Hood's Bay and Whitby. Bus 93 stops at the campsite gates all year round.

OPEN Start of March–end of October.

THE DAMAGE Adult £8–£10 (depending on the season) per night; child (3–15yrs) £3; electrical hook-ups £3–£4 (depending on the season).

Runswick Bay Camping

Hinderwell Lane, Runswick Bay, Whitby, North Yorkshire TS13 5HR   01947 840997   runswickbaycaravanandcampingpark.co.uk

Enjoying a fabulous location midway between Whitby and Staithes on the pristine North Yorkshire Coast, on the edge of the North York Moors National Park, Runswick Bay is a small village clutching the slopes of a sweeping bay. Narrow lanes weave between the red-roofed houses, past the thatched coastguard's cottage and down to the pristine sandy beach. At its edges, children armed with colourful nets clamber on the rocks, their crabbing hotspot framed by Lingrow Knowle, a lofty crag towering high above. Buckets fill with captured crustaceans as parents roll up their towels for the steep walk back to their hilltop destination: Runswick Bay Camping Park.

This convivial campsite has a mix of glamping, some hardstandings and a spacious tent camping field with around 70 grass pitches, 32 of which have electrical hook-ups. Glamping comes by way of a series of beautifully furnished wooden cabins, proper beds and heating, plus a firepit and a supply of wood and kindling. The site has a scattering of mains water taps with a well-maintained sanitary block in the centre. Its exposed hilltop position is remedied by trees around the border, which provide shelter from the wind, while gaps in the greenery reveal breathtaking views inland across the North York Moors.

The campsite is dog friendly, as is the whole of Runswick Bay, with a pet-welcoming pub just around the corner that serves tasty grub and local cask ales. From here it's an easy tumble down the steep lane to the beautiful sandy beach – perfect for amateur fossil-hunters wandering the Jurassic coastline and once again perfect for your four-legged friend to romp on. Those hoping to leave the car behind can trek the Cleaveland Way north to the artsy old fishing village of Staithes, where stone houses huddle around a picturesque harbour. Or head south to Whitby – an essential stop for visitors to the North Yorkshire Coast. The latter is a 15-minute drive or a half-day's walk.

Runswick Bay Camping Park is certainly a site that owes a lot to its surroundings, but the splendour of the place itself is also worth mentioning. Owners Jim and Caroline are wonderfully welcoming hosts, the facilities are extensive and very well looked after, and the onsite office is a helpful place to grab a bottle of milk or ask about local attractions. In short, Runswick Bay is the complete camping package – a congenial and scenic space to pitch the tent or glamp in style, with a wealth of things to see and do practically on your doorstep.

COOL FACTOR A welcoming spot in a friendly harbour village with a sheltered beach and access to the North York Moors.

WHO'S IN Everyone! Glampers, tents, caravans, campervans, families, groups, rallies, school groups...

ON SITE 45 spaces for tents and a further 32 with electricity, plus some hardstandings. A shower block, a wash house, a disabled shower/toilet, laundry facilities and a fridge/freezer for ice. The onsite office sells local produce and a few camping essentials. There's a small wooded area that's great for kids. Two glamping cabins are also available.

OFF SITE Runswick Bay beach, at the foot of the village, is the most immediate attraction, flanked by high rocky outcrops. The long-distance Cleveland Way passes the coast here and can be followed north to Staithes, a pretty harbour village backed by the severe headland of Cowbar Nab. Go out fishing or foraging with the brilliant Real Staithes outfit (01947 840278), run by local fisherman Sean and his wife Tricia, or take one of their immersive local tours of the village. Seven miles south, Whitby and its famous 199 steps lead up to the ruins of Whitby Abbey (01947 603568). Here attractions like The Captain Cook Memorial Museum (01947 601900) and The Dracula Experience (01947 601923) offer plenty to do as, of course, does the beach. Inland, the North Yorkshire Moors National Park (01439 770657) provides inexhaustible trails, footpaths and outdoors activities.

FOOD & DRINK The onsite office sells local produce such as bacon, eggs, milk and ice-creams, plus the village shop sells other groceries. Within walking distance, pubs like The Runswick Bay Hotel (01947 841010) and The Royal (01947 840215) serve local ales and good food, while the Cliffmount Hotel (01947 840103) offers fine dining. Within a mile there is also the The Badger Hounds at Hinderwell (01947 841774) an excellent pub on the way to Staithes that serves great food and welcomes both tired dogs and dog-walkers in the bar.

GETTING THERE From the north, take the A171 out of Guisbrough and follow the road across the hills until you're greeted by a panoramic view of Whitby and the sea. Keep following the road all the way, until you see a sign for Runswick Bay. Follow this and, at the end of the road, turn left at The Runswick Bay Hotel and the campsite is on the right. From the south and west, follow the A64 from York, then take the A169 from Malton, through Pickering and then across the North York Moors. Stay on the A169 all the way down Blue Bank, through Sleights, and up the other side of the valley to a roundabout where you should follow signs to Sandsend. Carry on all the way through untill you see Runswick Bay to your right. Turn right and go to the end of the road. Turn left at The Runswick Bay Hotel. The campsite is down the slope on the right.

PUBLIC TRANSPORT There are decent rail links to both Whitby to the south and Saltburn to the north, and the direct bus service that links the two towns stops outside the campsite gates or at The Runswick Bay Hotel.

OPEN All year (except January).

THE DAMAGE Adults £13; children (4–14yrs) £6.50; infants (2–3yrs) £3.50; under-1s free. Dogs £1.50.

Serenity Camping

High Street, Hinderwell, Whitby, North Yorkshire TS13 5JH   01947 841122   serenitycamping.co.uk

The sleepy, seaside settlement of Hinderwell on the North Yorkshire coast is a real village of old. Children stroll to the public tennis courts, a local notice board advertises church groups and community gatherings and two excellent pubs compete for your custom along the high street. There's a local butcher, a chippie and a village hall that hosts kids' parties and other local events, plus of course, the staple of any village that's truly worth a visit… a good campsite.

Hinderwell's campsite reflects the traditional, old-world charm of the village itself, focusing on simple pleasures and with a peaceful, timeless atmosphere. The village, meanwhile, plods along at an equally relaxed and homely pace – a welcoming environment for any visitor. Its name comes from the 5th century tale of St Hilda, who touched the ground and produced a spring that still flows from Hilda's Well today. The name of the campsite, you quickly realise, is equally as literal.

Silence is golden and this is very much the mantra at Serenity, which caters for a more relaxed and calm crowd than the usual seaside campers. Peace and quiet reign. There is the odd exception to the rule; the working smallholding next door supplies the sound of the odd tractor or cockerel crow but it only adds to the old-world charisma of the place, which is otherwise blessed with snooze-in-the-sun tranquillity most of the time.

The site itself has space for 40 tents and 19 caravans. Glampers, meanwhile, can choose from a cool Lotus Belle tent, a new boutique shepherd's hut or the private 'Potting Shed' – a large wooden cabin sleeping two with a private garden and uninterrupted sunset views. Warm, modern facilities feature alongside eco-friendly products, potted plants and a steady supply of fresh eggs from wandering hens, while a seat next to the pretty wildlife pond is perfect for whiling away the hours feeding the ducks and ducklings who visit every summer.

A number of the best local walks start directly from the campsite and it's less than a mile to the sands of Runswick Bay (see p.110–12). A particular highlight is heading out to the cliffs on the coastal footpath to Whitby, a wind-blown eight-mile route with stunning views. It's a mile north along the Cleveland Way to picturesque Staithes, too, home to a thriving artistic community with several galleries and craft shops. The village boasts seafaring myth, triumph, tragedy and even its own dialect – which is celebrated at the annual Staithes Arts and Heritage festival in September and all year round at the quirky Captain Cook and Staithes Heritage Museum. It's also the most unbeatable spot for enjoying seafood with the obligatory harbour view – try The Cod and Lobster pub, with benches outside.

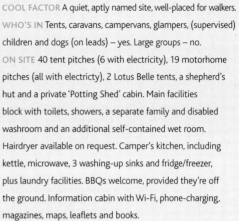

COOL FACTOR A quiet, aptly named site, well-placed for walkers.

WHO'S IN Tents, caravans, campervans, glampers, (supervised) children and dogs (on leads) – yes. Large groups – no.

ON SITE 40 tent pitches (6 with electricity), 19 motorhome pitches (all with electricty), 2 Lotus Belle tents, a shepherd's hut and a private 'Potting Shed' cabin. Main facilities block with toilets, showers, a separate family and disabled washroom and an additional self-contained wet room. Hairdryer available on request. Camper's kitchen, including kettle, microwave, 3 washing-up sinks and fridge/freezer, plus laundry facilities. BBQs welcome, provided they're off the ground. Information cabin with Wi-Fi, phone-charging, magazines, maps, leaflets and books.

OFF SITE A number of good walks run directly past the site – choose from clifftop routes or venture into the neighbouring oak woodland. The beautiful dog-friendly beach at Runswick Bay (see p.110) is a mile from the campsite, or head to the fishing village of Staithes for pubs and restaurants, as well as a small heritage museum (01947 841454). Dotty's Tearoom & Vintage Shop (01947 841096) is a must stop at Staithes, while there's plenty of unique tours and fishing expeditions to enjoy. A little further afield, at Grosmont, you'll find the historic North Yorkshire Moors Steam Railway, a wonderfully old-fashioned way of travelling between Whitby and Pickering (01751 472508).

FOOD & DRINK A short walk from the site, R. Lyth & Son (01947 840288), the local butcher, can supply you with BBQ packs, pies and breakfast rolls. The Runcible Spoon (01947 840700) is a great bistro nextdoor serving coffee, cake and lunch by day and evening meals at the weekend, sometimes accompanied by live music.

GETTING THERE The campsite is situated on the A174 between Whitby and Saltburn, just opposite the Badger Hounds pub in the village of Hinderwell.

PUBLIC TRANSPORT There is a regular daytime bus service from Whitby or Saltburn, stopping right outside the campsite.

OPEN March–October.

THE DAMAGE A tent and 2 people from £22 per night. Glamping accommodation from £70 per night.

Hemscott Hill Farm

Hemscott Hill Farm, Widdrington, Morpeth, Northumberland NE61 5EQ   01670 458118   hemscotthill.com

A pop-up campsite nestled in the undulating dunes that fringe seven-mile-long Druridge Bay, Hemscott Hill Farm is perhaps Northumberland's most unassuming patch from which to admire the North Sea's perma-choppy beauty. Combining the thrill of off-grid camping with epic coastal views (and a few basic facilities to smooth out the rough of the wild camping experience), this marram-dotted landscape is an utter joy. What meagre facilities exist for campers are basic but perfectly clean and functional – there are compost loos, a washing-up and kitchen shelter and cold showers for use, while if you walk the five minutes to the Hemscott Hill farmyard, you'll also find proper flushing loos and hot showers.

The walk to the yard itself takes you through the evolution of the dunes; from the sand, sea sponge and spiky marram grass near the beach, through to thicker vegetation and on to the meadows of the farm (geography students take note!). And while, across Hemscott's many acres, there is ample space for guests to savour, there's a great intimacy here that belies the farm's proximity to the sprawling peaks and valleys of Northumberland National Park.

If anywhere deserves the accolade 'a walker's paradise' it's right here on the coast. Venture in any direction from Hemscott for spectacular strolls; from the fossil-strewn beach at Hauxley to the many ancient castles that dot the northern stretch (Northumberland has more than any other county in England). And as dusk descends, stoke up the campfire and enjoy the dazzling sunsets as they yield to the UK's darkest night skies.

COOL FACTOR Off-grid camping on the wild and beautiful Northumberland coast.

WHO'S IN Tents, small campervans, groups – yes. Caravans, motorhomes, dogs – no.

ON SITE 40 pitches in 2 areas of the dunes along a 7-mile stretch of beach, plus a shepherd's hut for glamping at the farm. Furnished bell tents can also be hired. Off-grid facilities include compost loos, washing up sheds and cold showers in the field, with proper flushing loos and hot showers often available at the farm (a 5-minute walk away; not available when the farm is hosting weddings or special events). Fires and BBQs fine, as long as they are raised off the ground.

OFF SITE Easy access to miles of golden sands stretching from the 2 beaches at Amble in the north to Cresswell Beach in the south, best explored via the Northumberland Coast Path. The farm is also on the stunning Coast & Castles National Cycle Route No. 1. Small on gradient but big on scenery, heading north, this easily rideable path takes in Warkworth Castle (01665 711423), Bamburgh Castle (01668 214515) the Dunstanburgh Castle (01665 576231). You can hire bikes from Breeze Bikes (01665 710323) in Amble.

FOOD & DRINK The Widdrington Inn (01670 760260) and The Plough (01670 860 340) in Ellington are decent locals serving hearty pub grub. For tasty homebaked treats, it's a ¾-mile stroll to The Drift Café (01670 861599) in the dunes outside Cresswell. It's also a second-hand bookshop.

GETTING THERE Leave the A1 at the Chevington Moor exit and follow the road to the roundabout at Widdrington Village. Go straight across towards Druridge village and after 2 miles, at Druridge Bay National Trust Car Park, follow the road sharply to the right. Hemscott Hill Farm is ½ mile further along.

OPEN August–early September.

THE DAMAGE Camping from £15 per night. 2-night minimum stay on weekends (3-night minimum on Bank Holidays).

Walkmill Campsite

Near Guyvance, Warkworth, Northumberland NE65 9AJ   01665 710155   walkmillcampsite.co.uk

If ever a campsite fitted the *Cool Camping* criteria, then surely it is this hidden pocket of Northumberland, which ticks all our boxes relating to 'atmosphere', 'vibe' and of course the all-important location – set in 10 acres of grassland, surrounded by enchanting woodland and the weaving River Coquet.

"We promote camping in a natural, non-commercial environment", is how owner Claire describes Walkmill, and given the site's pleasing lack of evening entertainment and plastic playgrounds, we think that's a fitting description. The riverside pitches have vast amounts of space, shared only by the lambs and sheep at selected times of the year (though, sadly, due to fishing rules, access to the water isn't permitted), and give these places a real sense of 'wild camping', albeit with decent facilities that are always clean and tidy.

When you finally tire of Walkmill (if you ever do), the wild Northumberland coast is right on your doorstep. Stretching 64 miles north of Newcastle up to the Scottish border, this dramatic landscape is loaded with impressive sights, from the sturdy fortresses at nearby Warkworth and Alnwick to delightful villages strung along miles of wide, sandy beaches that you just might have all to yourself. A real attraction is Walkmill's abundance of wildlife, both on land and in the river. Swans, otters, herons and kingfishers lounge lazily by the riverbank; kestrels, buzzards and owls dominate the skies; while sharp-eyed campers have also spotted the odd badger. All in all it's a little spot of camping solace and will do a world of good for anyone looking to unwind.

COOL FACTOR Refreshingly understated private camping near Warkworth beach and castle.

WHO'S IN Tents, caravans, campervans, kids and dogs – yes.

ON SITE 10 tent pitches on a flat area beside the river at the bottom of a sloping field, plus 9 pitches (on the top level) available for caravans and motorhomes. Walkmill's static caravan acts as an information centre and bathroom, with a hot shower, bath and 2 toilets. 2 further toilets are located adjacent to the caravan, plus there are sinks, a microwave, fridge/freezer and kettle. Firepits are available for hire. Fishing day passes are available for the Coquet (salmon and trout).

OFF SITE From the top of the private farm track it's a pleasant 30-minute walk to Warkworth Castle (01665 711423), whose impressive cross-shaped keep, rising above the River Coquet, dominates one of the strongest fortresses in England, with a virtually intact circuit of towered walls. Beyond, walk to Warkworth Beach, home to Northside Surf School (07944 398115), who offer year-round surfing lessons for all abilities.

FOOD & DRINK Know your Knickerbocker from your Neapolitan? Then you'll love Spurelli (01665 710890), a boutique ice-cream makers in nearby Amble, located within The Old Chandlery. Customers can stay and watch the world go by from the outside seating area. Amble is also home to small convenience stores and a Sunday market. There are several larger supermarkets in Alnwick (a 15-minute drive).

GETTING THERE From Warkworth, take the first left immediately after the bridge. Follow the road for a mile, over a railway crossing, and turn left towards Guyzance Brotherwick. Drive past Brotherwick Farm and continue for another ½ mile. Turn left at the bend, up and over a small stone railway bridge, and turn immediately right on to the farm track to Walkmill.

OPEN March–October.

THE DAMAGE Adults £7.50, teens (13–17yrs) £5, children (2–12yrs) £3, under-2s free. Additional cars £1.

Ravenglass Campsite

Ravenglass Camping and Caravanning Club, Ravenglass, Cumbria CA18 1SR   01229 717250   campingandcaravanningclub.co.uk

With no less than 16 beautiful lakes squeezed between England's tallest mountains across a mere 30-odd miles, The Lake District is Britain's most hyped scenic area, and with good reason. Its landscape of tranquil water, impressive valleys and charming stone-built villages has been drawing artists, writers and lovers of the outdoors for centuries. Recently crowned a UNESCO World Heritage Site, there's unlikely to be any let-up in its popularity any time soon. So thank goodness there are plenty of excellent campsites on hand.

Set on the outskirts of Ravenglass, a pretty Roman fishing village on the Lake District's west coast, this Camping and Caravanning Club Site combines modern facilities with old-school camping principles. The world's oldest camping club has taken care in creating a site where the facilities – a modern shower block and a well-stocked shop – don't come at the expense of its natural surroundings. And what surroundings! With six acres of mature woodland lying just 500 metres from the dramatic Cumbrian coast, this unique destination is a walker's paradise.

And who's welcome? Well, everyone really. Ravenglass accommodates up to 75 caravans, motorhomes and canvas campers. In fact traditional tenters shouldn't be put off by the number of caravans allowed; the camping area is situated in a peaceful, tree-lined section of the site. Also, located in another wooded area (en route to the main field) there are three camping pods – cosy alternatives made from locally sourced timber and insulated with wool – along with a couple of new, pre-pitched and furnished safari tents, well-suited to families who don't want to over-fill the car with camping clobber.

Given a few days you could easily see most of the Lake District's most popular attractions. You could try a circuit taking in the towns of Windermere, Ambleside and Bowness, Wordsworth's Dove Cottage in Grasmere, and the dramatic northern scenery of Keswick and Ullswater, although to be honest some of the best scenery is right on your doorstep – in the breathtaking valleys of Eskdale and Langdale. The estuary village of Ravenglass is also the access point for the open-to-the-elements Ravenglass & Eskdale Railway, without doubt one of the most scenic narrow-gauge railway routes in the country and one of the oldest too. Puffing its way inland for around seven miles, through spectacular valleys, it's a great route further into the National Park.

The local coastline is perhaps the very best place to start any weekend's exploring, however. While the vast space of the Lake District allows anyone to walk, explore and revel in the views without worrying about their busy lives, it is here, in it's western-most corner, that arguably the quietest, most undiscovered (and underrated) aspects of the National Park are found. From the wildlife that flourishes in the estuary to the peaceful picnic benches overlooking the silt and sand Ravenglass Beach, there are few finer places to enjoy both mountains and sea in one fell swoop.

74

COOL FACTOR Six acres of woodlands and only 500m from the seafront.

WHO'S IN Tents, caravans, motorhomes, kids, dogs and non-Camping & Caravanning Club members – yes. Big groups – no.

ON SITE 75 pitches, 56 of which are hardstanding with electric hook-ups. 3 camping pods for hire. Showers, family shower room, flushing toilets, washbasins and electric-shaver sockets. Dedicated accessible facilities, chemical toilet disposal point, motorhome stop-off, dishwashing facilities and shop. Payphone, drinking water taps, washing machines, ice-pack freezing, gas cylinders and Wi-Fi.

OFF SITE The site sits on the edge of the picturesque village of Ravenglass and is just a short stroll along a wooded lane from the sea shore. Ravenglass is the only coastal village in the Lake District National Park, and stands at the meeting point of three rivers flowing from the Lakeland's most majestic fells. The village and surrounding area are steeped in history and were once a Roman port – the remains of a Roman bath house are down the lane from the campsite. The Hadrian's Cycle Way starts at Ravenglass and the Cumbria Coastal Way passes right by the campsite. The local area also boasts England's highest mountain, deepest lake and smallest church, with 'Britain's favourite view' at Wastwater and Scafell Pike a short drive away. The Eskdale Valley stretches from the west coast through to the foot of Hardknot Pass and you can take a trip on the Ravenglass & Eskdale Railway, a narrow gauge railway that runs through this stunning valley.

FOOD & DRINK The licensed, onsite shop sells local meat from Wilson's Butchers (01946 820036) and locally brewed beers. There are 3 pubs in Ravenglass (all within walking distance). The family-friendly Ratty Arms (01229 717676) offers a range of tasty pub grub dishes and hosts a weekly quiz night and frequent music events.

GETTING THERE From the south, leave the M6 at the South Lakes turnoff. At the roundabout, take the first exit to Barrow on to the A590 for 20 miles. Turn right at the A5092 to Whitehaven and Workington for 30 miles (this road becomes the A595). Turn left towards Ravenglass and the site is well signposted on the left. From the north leave the M6 at junction 40 and follow the A66 west to Workington for 34 miles. Take the A595 to Whitehaven and drive past Whitehaven, Egremont and Gosforth for 25 miles. Turn right towards Ravenglass and the site is well signposted on the left.

PUBLIC TRANSPORT Ravenglass' old railway station and the nearest bus stop are both 500m from the campsite.

OPEN February–November, plus the Christmas school holidays.

THE DAMAGE Pitch and 2 people from £20.80–£35. Add £3.85 for electricity per night and £4.85 for a hardstanding with electricity. Pods from £43.75 a night.

Hiring a Campervan

If there's one sure-fire way of spicing up your camping trip it's leaving the family car at home and taking a set of shiny new wheels.

No matter how many years you spent playing games of Tetris in your youth, packing the family car is never an easy task, especially with rigid cool-boxes, clumsy camping stoves and a collection of fold-out camping chairs to mould into the boot. Bags are covering the rear windscreen, beach balls are blocking the view and are those someone's knees prodding you in the back?

While nothing beats a classic night under canvas, the compact, ergonomic and economical nature of a campervan gives it a special place in the camping pantheon. While you've been bungee-cording water containers to your roof rack and stock-piling bottles of camping gas, an entire team of engineers have gone into designing the fridge in the latest VW campervan. And with less time spent pitching the tent, a van gives you more time to fully explore the coastline, too.

Halfway between tent camping and travelling around in a miniature, moveable holiday home, campervans provide all the fun of a regular camping experience but with added weatherproof insurance and an extra element of excitement. After all, nothing can turn a fully grown adult into a kid at Christmas quite like putting them behind the wheel of a vintage VW campervan.

In keeping with the *Cool Camping* ethos, we've steered well clear of colossal Winnebagos and avoided all things caravan, recommending only the best campervan hire companies in the UK. Stylish and perfectly formed, the campervans they hire out are ideally suited to family holidays on bendy British roads and represent just a few of the companies we recommend on coolcamping.com. Visit our website for more vans, more locations and more road-tripping inspiration.

Big Tree Campervans

Based in a small Perthshire village in the heart of Scotland's 'Big Tree Country', this family-run enterprise has a fleet of eight different vans, with room for five when driving and sleeping space for four. Along with their principal location, the Yearsley family can arrange pick-up and drop-off of the vans at the main airports – Edinburgh, Glasgow and Dundee – so you can head straight off into the Highlands. There's a dog-friendly van available too. Bring your pooch along or just steal Bob the affable Big Tree dog.

Bankfoot, Perthshire; 01738 788056;
bigtreecampervans.com

Indie Campers

These guys are the big guns. With more than 50 pick-up locations in Europe, including most major cities, they're the go-to campervan hire company if you're heading to a beach abroad. They've got a diverse fleet of vehicles that includes the new VW California or – for a cool, surfing-themed paint job – a Fiat Ducato. All feature fixed or rollaway double beds and a whole host of handy extras that come as standard, such as bedding kit, cooking kit, portable cooker and an electric cooler. Best of all, with regional experts at each depot, you can get your bearings and reccommendations abroad before you hit the road (on the correct side).

55 pick-up locations across the UK and Europe, including most major airports; 01776 240031; indiecampers.com

CamperVantastic

Founded in 2006 by Steve and Kate Lumley, London-based CamperVantastic have fast become the UK's premier, multi-award-winning VW California campervan hire specialists. The well-travelled couple met as keen backpackers and will quickly put you at ease in the vehicles – modern VW California and California Beach campervans with plenty of pop-top space and all the 21st-century gadgetry you need. For an active beach holiday they can provide you with that all-important surf-board rack, along with other extras that include bike racks, drive-away awnings, luxury bedding sets and more. The only hard part? Avoiding the traffic out of London.

Stanstead Road, Lewisham, London; 020 8291 6800;
campervantastic.com

Bunk Campers

If you want to avoid the classic caravan cliché, then Bunk Campers, who renew their fleet every three years, is certainly the company to use. There's nothing vintage about their eight different vehicle models and, while some are large motorhome-type abodes, the smaller, more compact vans still afford plenty of space for families, too. Already one of the best-known campervan hire companies in Ireland, they have bases in Edinburgh and Glasgow (airport pick-up available) and a depot at London Gatwick.

Five locations across the UK; including Edinburgh, Glasgow, Belfast and London Gatwick; 028 9081 3057; bunkcampers.com

Van Kampers

Van Kampers have just one campervan for hire, a new, Brazilian-built VW that has been designed to replicate the style of the classic 70s model but packs an economical petrol engine inside. The result gets you top prizes for style but also some peace of mind when it comes to reliability. The pop-top roof accommodates a cool platform bed that's ideal for children and teenagers, while the seats below fold down to become a double bed for parents. An extra awning sleeps an additional two people. Best of all, it's just two miles from pick-up in Pembrokeshire to the nearest beach.

Mathry, Haverfordwest, Pembrokeshire; 01348 837994; vankampers.co.uk

LandCruise Motorhome Hire

If you want to pull out all the stops, LandCruise – the biggest supplier of rental motorhomes on the South Coast – offer the closest thing you can get to a hotel on wheels. When it comes to the interiors, think family-sized yacht – long sofas, digital televisions, central heating, air conditioning, a plush en suite bathroom and shiny, fully equipped kitchen. At over six metres in length (apart from one model), these are not tiny campervans for even tinier rural lanes, but if you've got the confidence of a truck driver and a family in need of ample space then take your pick. There's a reason that they're the number one supplier on the patch.

Oving, Chichester, West Sussex; 01243 380000; landcruise.uk.com

Trwyn Yr Wylfa

Conway Old Road, Penmaenmawr, Conwy LL34 6SF   01492 650672   coastalview-camping-conwy-northwales.co.uk

Many campsites boast 'views to die for', but few can lay claim to the scenic vistas enjoyed by visitors to Trwyn Yr Wylfa. With mountains to one side and a seascape to the other, this Conwy coast campsite's location takes some beating.

Though in business since the 1940s, Trwyn Yr Wylfa was recently acquired by the folks behind Cefn Cae – a popular *Cool Camping* spot in Snowdonia. Like Cefn Cae, the peaceful farm setting here plays host to just a scattering of pitches and the set-up is refreshingly understated compared to some of the other more commercial holiday parks along this coast. It's very much a campers' campsite here, and the resulting clientele are a friendly mix of families, couples and walkers, with stag and hen parties and other large party groups outlawed.

Wherever you decide to pitch your tent on the site, uninterrupted views are promised. To the west, Anglesey, Puffin Island and the Menai Straits; to the east, Llandudno and The Great Orme headland; to the south, the slopes of the Carneddau mountains. On the very clearest of days, you might just spy the Isle of Man across the Irish Sea to the north. It comes as little surprise, then, that *Trwyn yr Wylfa* translates as 'watching point'.

But it isn't all about whiling away the hours transfixed by the scenery. The site's location on the northern fringes of Snowdonia National Park, means there are plenty of walking routes to enjoy – plus local amenities are also easily reachable, with both beach and pubs a few minutes' stroll away.

COOL FACTOR Sandwiched between beach and mountains... surely the tastiest kind of sandwich there is.

WHO'S IN Tents, campervans, caravans, dogs – yes. Large groups – no.

ON SITE 70 grass camping pitches and 2 pre-pitched bell tents. Wash-block dispensing hot showers with separate ladies' and gents' facilities, a dish-washing area and a large, kid-friendly playing field for ball games. Communal kitchen with microwave, fridge and freezer. Indoor washing-up area. Laundry facilities available (for a small charge). Chemical toilet disposal. Free guest Wi-Fi available and good 3G coverage.

OFF SITE It's a 15-minute walk to sand and pebble Penmaenmawr beach – Blue Flag-approved and nicely landscaped, with terraces, flower borders and grassed areas. Behind is a café, outdoor paddling pool and kids' play area. The cycle- and walking-friendly North Wales Path can be accessed directly from the campsite. Take the stretch over the Synchant Pass and Conwy Mountain (*Mynydd y Dref* in Welsh) to the UNESCO-listed Conwy Castle & Walls (01492 592358).

FOOD & DRINK Penmaenmawr's Beach Café (01492 623883) does a decent fry-up with views over the Menai Strait to Anglesey. The Village Bistro (01492 622323) offers a range of light lunches and hearty meals, such as burgers, pasta dishes and steaks. The Gladstone (01492 623231) is 400 yards from the site, serves wholesome pub grub, boasts a beautiful beer garden and comes CAMRA-approved for ale aficionados.

GETTING THERE For sat-navs, enter LL34 6SF. At Puffin Roundabout, take the first exit on to Conway Road heading to Penmaenmawr. Turn left on to Church Road, then left on to Conway Old Road. The campsite is on your right.

OPEN March–October.

THE DAMAGE A pitch and 2 people from £18. Adults £5, children (3–16yrs) £2.50, under-3s free.

Aberafon

Gyrn Goch, Caernarfon, Gwynedd LL54 5PN   01286 660295   aberafon.co.uk

Let us not beat about the bush – this campsite scores highly on the old 'location, location, location' rating situated, as it is, in a beautiful spot between the beach and mountains of the Llyn Peninsula, 10 miles south of Caernarfon. Negotiating a steep, narrow path to the site, past a bubbling stream, feels like you are descending into a secret valley within the mountains. Drive past a covered games room and the owners' lovely house, past rows of white tourers and down to a joyous coastal 'Beach Field', a grassy patch so close to the sea as to be virtually in it. It can only be accessed by small vehicles and features 16 pitches with seven electrical hook-ups.

Both grassy tiers of the campsite sharply meet the rugged coastline, where there is a tiny, partly sandy, wild beach full of rockpools to explore. Braver swimmers might attempt a quick dip – wild swimming is all part of Aberafon's package – but there are sandier swimming beaches along the peninsula. There is even a slipway to launch your sailing boat from, should you happen to carry one with you. Bringing canoes and kayaks is a better bet, or you can try wakeboarding at the local sporting venue, Glasfryn Park, near Pwllheli. Then, of course, there's walking on the coastal path or up into the hills behind. Co-owner Hugh has regularly jumped off nearby Gyrn Goch mountain, which overlooks the campsite, strapped to a paraglider. If you're feeling equally adventurous, sign up with the local paragliding school. Otherwise, just let the kids safely enjoy their seaside surroundings: happy kids make happy parents, after all.

COOL FACTOR A fantastic isolated seaside situation, where children can enjoy real independence as they explore.

WHO'S IN Families, tents, campervans, caravans, dogs – yes. Groups – no.

ON SITE 65 pitches overall, for tents and tourers. 40 hook-ups. Campfires permitted on the beach, wood available to buy. Clean but basic facilities – 1 shower/toilet block, with 13 toilets, 6 showers (3 male/female), 4 urinals. Laundry facilities, dishwasher, ice-pack freezing, TV and pool room. Onsite shop for daily essentials (open during the school summer holiday only). BBQs are permitted but must be raised off the ground.

OFF SITE There's all sorts happening nearby, including the historic and rather quaint town of Caernarfon, with its awesome castle (01286 677617), and the Welsh Highland Railway, which steams from Caernarfon (01286 677018) all the way to Porthmadog through the mountains. The atmospheric Llechwedd Slate Caverns (01766 83036) are also a must-see, whilst Penrhyn Castle at Bangor (01248 353084) is decadence on a massive scale. A bit nearer is the eccentric Caernarfon Airworld Museum (01286 830800), located on the former Royal Air Force station at Llandwrog.

FOOD & DRINK The nearest supermarket is a mile away in Clynnog Fawr. Drive across the peninsula and treat yourself to some fine dining at the Plas Bodegroes (01758 612363) in Pwllheli.

GETTING THERE Take the A487 from Caernarfon south towards Porthmadog for 4 miles, then the A499 towards Pwllheli for 7 miles, then take a sharp right turn into the very narrow lane at Gyrn Goch.

PUBLIC TRANSPORT A regular bus service (0871 200 22 33) runs to/from Caernarfon, Porthmadog, Pwllheli and Nefyn.

OPEN Easter–end September.

THE DAMAGE Adults £8.50, children (3–15yrs) £4.25, under-3s free. Electrical hook-ups £3.50. Boat on trailer £4.

Mynydd Mawr

Llanllawen Fawr, Aberdaron, Pwllheli, Gwynedd LL53 8BY   01758 760223   aberdaroncaravanandcampingsite.co.uk

Situated at the far western tip of the Llyn Peninsula, it almost seems as though Mynydd Mawr lies on the very edge of the known world. In glorious isolation, it is sheltered from the prevailing winds, but has a stunning view out across to Bardsey Island. Once upon a time the island was an important pilgrimage destination and it was thought that a quick trip across the water to it could save your soul. They obviously knew a thing or two back then because, in our busy world, a camping pilgrimage to Mynydd Mawr could very well do the same job.

This out-of-the-way place rarely gets crowded; the site is small, the rugged scenery massive, and there is an overwhelming feeling of being hugged by Mother Nature. One of the most noticeable things about this place is the silence, or more accurately the lack of artificial noise. Of course you can hear the sea, the birds and the wind, but the lack of cars, aeroplanes, and even boats has an unusually soothing – and welcome – effect. Listening to the silence may seem like an odd thing to do, but at Mynydd Mawr campsite you just can't help yourself.

If late-evening strolls are your thing then Mynydd Mawr is just the place to be. The walk from the campsite to the westernmost extremity of the Llyn to watch the sun plunge into the red western sky is one of life's finest pleasures. The Llyn Peninsula Coastal Path passes the site and offers you the opportunity to stride off along the edge of the world to Aberdaron in one direction or to Porth Oer in the other. Aberdaron has a café or two, a pub, a nice beach, a quaint little

church and the chance to get on a boat to visit Bardsey Island. To call Aberdaron a resort would be ludicrous but, after the isolation of Mynydd Mawr, it feels almost like re-entry into the world. You can even buy an ice-cream there and get free Wi-Fi on the beach. The walk to Porth Oer along the northern and western fringe exposes you to a much bigger and wilder landscape, with 240 metre cliffs plunging into the restless waters, while Porth Oer itself, about four very rough miles away, is a soft, inviting place of golden sands.

The Llyn Peninsula isn't the kind of place to go if you're seeking bright lights and entertainment, and Mynydd Mawr lies at the very bottom of this scenic cul-de-sac, so getting anywhere at all will never be achieved quickly on the narrow, bumpy roads. But wherever you venture on the lovely Llyn, returning to Mynydd Mawr for that sunset stroll – and listening again to that sound of silence – is a haunting and thoroughly evocative experience. And one that is not to be missed.

COOL FACTOR Total peace and quiet at the very tip of the 30-mile-long Llyn Peninsula.

WHO'S IN Tents, campervans, caravans, motorhomes, well-behaved dogs (on a lead) – yes. Big noisy groups – no.

ON SITE Facilities (recently refurbished) comprise ladies' and gents' toilets and showers, plus disabled access and family facilities. There are 2 washing-up areas and a freezer for ice packs, plus several scattered water points. Chemical disposal for caravans. Electrical hook-ups. There's also a cracking onsite café (see *Food & Drink*). Campfires are allowed but must be in a container and off the ground.

OFF SITE Hop on to the scenic coastal path or wander up the surrounding heather-strewn slopes. 1½ miles east, Aberdaron is a beautiful hamlet and the place to go for organised fishing trips, water sports or wildlife tours, while Whistling Sands beach is also nearby. Most boat trips, of course, head straight to Bardsey Island, a nature reserve and designated SSSI, and the centrepiece of the campsite's magnificent views. Trefor is slightly further and has a quiet sandy beach – another place where boats can be launched.

FOOD & DRINK The onsite café is something of a local legend – Carol's bacon butties are manna from heaven for early-rising campers, with breakfast, light lunches, afternoon teas, homemade cakes, ice-cream and more available. The Ship Inn (01758 760204), 2 miles away at Aberdaron, serves outstanding food in an intimate, front room-style setting.

GETTING THERE Take the B4413 to Aberdaron. After the 30mph sign take the first right to Uwchmynydd. Continue until you come to the second crossroads, also signed for Uwchmynydd, and seafood restaurant. Continue for a mile, passing the chapel and a row of whitewashed cottages. The campsite is the last stop before you reach the headland.

OPEN Easter–October.

THE DAMAGE From £10–£18 per unit. Electricity £2.

Nant-y-Bîg

Cilan, Abersoch, Pwllheli, Gwynedd LL53 7DB 01758 712686 nantybig.co.uk

A campsite with a view? You've heard it all before, right? However, the unforgettable scenery greeting campers upon arrival at Nant-y-Bîg is so much more than just a pleasant backdrop. This family-run, environmentally aware campsite is situated slap-bang on the Llyn Peninsula, a remarkable region known as the 'Edge of Wales' – and if you like living on the edge, you'll no doubt love pitching your tent in the fields of Nant-y-Bîg.

The first thing to decide is where to camp. Guests have three options. There's a section with electrical hook-ups (no coastline views here, but it's only a 10–15 minute walk to the beach); a second meadow has panoramic seaside views of Cardigan Bay, while there's also a third area just above the surf-friendly Porth Ceiriad beach. The majority of pitches are flat, well maintained and provide plenty of space for the kids to roam. Check the weather report upon arrival; if wind is predicted (and out on an pointy peninsula boy does it get windy!) ask for a more sheltered spot. Nant-y-Bîg's cheerful owner Dylan displays the latest forecast in his tastefully converted reception area, housed in one of the old farm stables.

Facilities here are simple but well looked after. There's a newish shower block and the toilets are kept clean, and although facilities aren't the reason campers visit this unique corner of Britain, the site isn't actually that far from civilisation. Abersoch (two miles away) comes alive in summer with an influx of surfers, boaties and beachbums. Fringed by lush green hills, the picturesque village has a decent selection of pubs, cafés and restaurants, with some overlooking the pretty harbour.

If you enjoy coastal walking then Nant-y-Bîg is your Eden. The relationship between the Llyn Peninsula's steep hills and seaside makes for intoxicating stuff. There's wildlife a-plenty – keep your eyes peeled for the bay's famous dolphins – and the peninsula is an important spot for migratory birds, in particular. But be warned: when Mother Nature gets herself in a bad mood, ramblers are a wee bit exposed, so make sure you bring a spare pair of socks and a waterproof jacket. That said, the weather can change quickly; and when the sun reappears, illuminating the full, broad blue of the Irish Sea, you'll be ever so glad you came to Nant-y-Bîg.

COOL FACTOR Space as endless as the view.

WHO'S IN Tents, campervans, motorhomes, caravans, dogs (on a lead at all times) – yes. Groups – no.

ON SITE Pitches spread across 3 large fields (2 with sea views). One is away from the sea but has the advantage of electrical hook-ups – with 8 showers, 6 toilets, 2 urinals and 8 washbasins, plus a dish-washing area. If you're more keen on the views, then the 'Panoramic' or 'Near the Beach' areas are the better picks, with only 60 pitches over 9 acres of land. Facilities are basic but always clean. The toilet block for the 'Panoramic' area is down behind reception and has 4 toilets, 6 toilets, 2 urinals and 4 washbasins. The 'Near the Beach' fields have a simple toilet block with 3 toilets, 3 washbasins and a urinal. BBQs permitted off the ground but no campfires. Coin-operated washing machine and tumble dryer. Ice-pack freezing, Wi-Fi and mobile phone-charging available.

OFF SITE Head west to the fishing village of Aberdaron, where the stone cottages are so spotless you could be forgiven for believing the village was freshly painted. Its 5th-century church of St Hywyn (01758 760659) comes steeped in Welsh history. Don't leave without peeking at the curious pair of carved stones displayed against the north-east wall – thought to be the gravestones of 2 early priests, Senacus and Veracius.

FOOD & DRINK The best local spots include The Sun Inn (01758 712660) and Zinc (01758 713433) in Abersoch – booking is recommended at the latter. Boasting views across Yr Eifl and Snowdonia, The Ty Coch Inn (01758 720498) is well worth the 30-minute drive but can then only be accessed by walking across the sands from Morfa Nefyn.

GETTING THERE From Sarn Bach, head towards Cilan and after 600m you will see a small green metal shed on your left; the turning for Nant-y-Bîg is 30m up the road.

PUBLIC TRANSPORT Pwllheli railway station is less than 10 miles away and a bus passes the end of the lane to Nant-y-Bîg 3 times a day.

OPEN Easter–end of October.

THE DAMAGE Adults £9, children (3–15yrs) £3, under-3s free. Dogs £2. Electricity £3.50.

Graig Wen

Arthog, Nr Dolgellau, Gwynedd LL39 1YP   01341 250482   graigwen.co.uk

Situated in the south-west corner of the Snowdonia National Park, there's no doubt that Graig Wen enjoys one of the best campsite locations in the whole of Wales. Set among some 45 acres of its own wild woods and meadows, and with amazing views over the Mawddach Estuary curling down to Cardigan Bay below, this established spot plays host to happy campers and ample wildlife alike. It's not surprising, then, that it has won the Green Snowdonia Award for 'Most Sustainable Campsite', along with a clutch of other gongs, including 'The Best Camping and Glamping Site' according to Go North Wales. Yet for all those awards, Graig Wen remains a wonderfully peaceful and unpretentious spot to stay.

At the heart of the campsite's success is its owners' passion to constantly improve the site while simultaneously preserving its wild nature. To accompany the grassy camping pitches, Sarah and John have hand-built two yurts from ash trees found on the land, kitting them out with quirky furniture and textiles, while two more pop-up yurts have been designed to move around the site depending on the season (closer to loos, showers and the comforts of electricity in winter time). There's also a cute wooden 'caban' with a Scandinavian feel – its glazed walls provide magnificent views but can be shuttered when needed – plus a bell tent and a holiday cottage. Really, the needs of every possible type of visitor are covered across the campsite.

In keeping with its award-winning status, Graig Wen's well-maintained facilities are kept spick and span, with hot showers and sparkling toilets and washbasins. Viewing benches overlooking the Mawddach Estuary offer the best seat in the house at sunset o'clock – especially given Snowdonia's 'International Dark Sky Reserve' status – and a simple camp shop stocks local ales and other essentials; you can also book breakfast hampers and chilled bubbly for your arrival. The pitches themselves are also positioned to suit most tastes, with space for tourers and tents as well as all the glamping options, and campfires are permitted in firepits.

A geocache trail provides a way of exploring the site's woods and streams, and learning a bit about the area's slate-mining heritage. More intrepid explorers, meanwhile, can tackle Cader Idris – the spectacular mountain at the back of Graig Wen, where the crowds tend to be much smaller than on the summit of Snowdon. According to legend, if you spend the night on the top of Cader Idris, you'll come down a poet or, yes, a madman.

You can also cycle all the way to the beaches at Fairbourne or Barmouth without even seeing a road, and virtually the entire route to Dolgellau in the other direction is road-free, too. In addition to the cycle track, there's another family cycling path, plus more challenging mountain-bike trails at nearby Coed-y-Brenin.

COOL FACTOR Smart, sustainable and quite simply, lush.

WHO'S IN Everyone! Tents, campervans, caravans, glampers, dogs, cyclists/mountain bikers, walkers...

ON SITE 10 hard electric pitches and 2 grass pitches on the top touring site and 18 grass pitches in the lower camping fields (3 with parking). Plus 4 yurts, a Welsh caban and a bell tent for hire in summer. Arrive 2–4pm for a lift to your pitch or wheelbarrows are provided to move your kit to the lower field pitches. There's a steep hill-climb to the shower and toilet facilities. Campfires are allowed on lower fields and there's a communal campfire on the top field. Bikes for hire.

OFF SITE Climbing nearby Cader Idris (892m) is a great option, and the family-friendly 'Pony Path' makes it manageable for all – the campsite give a certificate to all children who make the summit. Alternatively, walk straight from the site along the stunning (and flat) waterside Mawddach Trail to the seaside treats of Barmouth – go crabbing or visit Knickerbockers ice-cream parlour – or cycle and continue along the estuary to Fairbourne beach.

FOOD & DRINK The owners sell eggs, ice-cream, marshmallows and breakfast hampers (£30) in high season. Stock up on local produce in Dolgellau at the Country Market (Thursday morning) or the Farmer's Market (third Sunday of the month). Good pub grub (and views) at the George III Hotel (01341 422525), 5 minutes' drive or an hour's delightful walk along the estuary cycle trail.

GETTING THERE Turn off the A470 Dolgellau bypass on to the A493, signposted Tywyn-Fairbourne. The campsite is 4½ miles further on the right. Head from Fairbourne on the A493, through Arthog, past the quarry and look for a sign saying 'Concealed entrance' on the left – that's it.

PUBLIC TRANSPORT Morfa Mawddach train station is about 2 miles from the site, accessible by foot/cyclepath or bus. Buses run between Aberystwyth, Machynlleth and Dolgellau. Ask the driver to drop you off at Graig Wen.

OPEN All year (though it's worth calling ahead to check that the part of the campsite you want is open).

THE DAMAGE Adults £7–£9, children (5–16yrs) £3–£4; under-5s free. One-off vehicle charge (£10) for the tent fields. Glamping accommodation from £60 per night.

Cae Du Farm

Rhoslefain, Tywyn, Gwynedd LL36 9ND   01654 711234   caedufarmholidays.co.uk

'Away from it all', 'a wonderful sea view', 'an idyllic location' and 'well maintained' are all terms that can be fairly applied to Cae Du Farm. But to be honest none of these descriptions quite does the place justice, and your heart can't help but skip a beat or two when seeing this place for the first time. For there, a couple of hundred yards below, lying right next to the sea, with an unspoiled landscape enveloping the site, is the campsite of your dreams.

It looks like a place that has become detached from the real world, and in fact proves to be just that. Indeed, if all you want from your camping holiday is a sea view and an escape from the mad world we all live in, then this is the perfect place in which to unwind to the rhythms of the waves and the tides. 'Idyllic' is a word that is used far too often, but it sums up the situation of Cae Du Farm as no other word can.

But while Cae Du Farm provides an escape from the rat race, it isn't so far removed that there is nothing else to do when staring out to sea ceases to hold your attention. Or if the children start walking around with placards round their necks protesting their need for action. Or if the weather turns a bit wild on this exposed stretch of coastline – which it can do.

It is, after all, only a mile to the nearest train station, from where it's a short hop of three miles to link up with the very scenic Talyllyn Railway. There are all manner of destinations in the other direction, not least the small, time-warped seaside resort of Barmouth (Abermaw) to the north, which still has donkeys strolling the enormous

beach and colourful swingboats rocking back and forth. The Mawddach Trail, meanwhile, follows the course of another, disused, railway route from Morfa Mawddach near Fairbourne to Dolgellau, and is one of the most enchanting walks (or bike rides) anywhere in the area. As you cycle across the old bridge where mountain stream-fed river washes into Cardigan Bay, you can fully appreciate the mighty meeting of Snowdonia and the sea.

Indeed, despite the site's other-worldly location whatever you want from your camping break, you can be sure it won't be far from Cae Du Farm.

COOL FACTOR Incredible waterside location and a dish-washing view that would inspire even the most undomesticated camper.

WHO'S IN Tents, campervans, caravans, dogs – yes.

ON SITE Excellent facilities block with toilets, showers (£1), laundry, dish-washing facilities and 2 freezers for ice-blocks. No electrical hook-ups. Campfires permitted and wood sold onsite (£5 per bundle).

OFF SITE Bring bikes and hop on the excellent Mawddach Trail (see pp.140 & 143). Head north to the Llechwedd Slate Caverns where Zip World (01248 601444) has become hugely popular in recent years. Over 8km of wires are strung throughout the mountains providing a truly unique aerial experience. If it rains, there are several train rides nearby: from Tonfanau station, a mile south of the campsite, the scenic Cambrian Coast service (08457 484950) runs to Pwllheli in one direction and historic Shrewsbury in the other; and there's also the Fairbourne Railway (01341 250362) and Talyllyn Railway (01654 710472). Or if it's really pouring, head to the little cinema in Tywyn (01654 710260) and catch a film.

FOOD & DRINK Lamb burgers (made with farm-reared meat) are sold at the farmhouse. This isn't ideal pub-crawling territory, but 3 miles away in Llwyngwril The Garthangharad (01341 250484) is a lovely old, white-washed pub and restaurant with exposed beams and all the trinkets on show. Some 3 miles in the opposite direction, at Bryncrug, The Peniarth Arms (01654 711505) does decent pub grub, too, while a few miles further towards Dolgellau, at Penmaenpool, The George III Hotel (01341 422525) boasts a cosy bar, an exceptional restaurant and scenic location overlooking the Mawddach Estuary.

GETTING THERE From Tywyn follow signs to Bryncrug and, from there, take the coast road A493 towards Rhoslefain. The campsite is ½ mile further along the A493 on the left.

PUBLIC TRANSPORT Take the coastal rail service to Tonfanau then hop into a taxi or brave the mile-long walk on foot.

OPEN March–October.

THE DAMAGE 2 adults in a tent or small campervan £15, family tent and larger vans £20. Dogs £2.

Smugglers Cove Boatyard

Frongoch, Aberdyfi, Gwynedd LL35 0RG   01654 767842   smugglerscoveboatyard.co.uk

You'll never know the acoustics in the hull of a boat could be so perfect until you've tried it. A piano, tucked beneath the low beams of the main deck, is alive under the fingers of a particularly gifted musician and everyone else, clustered along rug-thrown benches, is belting out the chorus of "What shall we do with the drunken sailor?" Every verse seems to grow louder. At one point the guitar is even picked up for extra gusto, but it all peters out into laughter when the group runs out of lines.

Somewhere between a pub, party, village hall and your best mate's living room, this is just another night below deck aboard The Boy John – officially *Cool Camping*'s favourite ship. By the next day the partying pianists have left and a couple have taken a quieter captaincy of the vessel, kipping in the cabin where a double bed offers quirky but rustic glamping-esque accommodation.

Unique as it may be, though, The Boy John is just one feather in this unusual campsite's cap. Smugglers Cove Boatyard contains as many hidden gems as the name suggests and when you step from the hull of the boat out into the eye-blinkingly bright sunlight there is still a treasure trove to explore. This, after all, is not really a glamping site at all but an eclectic, rustic sustainable camping resource with a little bit of everything on offer.

Smugglers Cove Boatyard started life as an old slate works and quay overlooking the beautiful Dyfi Estuary. For years it continued its existence building boats, offering moorings and acting as a

hub for local sailors. But now, while these nautical trades continue, it has also opened its doors to fellow outdoor enthusiasts. Along the coastal footpath, a hundred metres from the boatyard, three individual camping pitches offer the very best spots on the Dyfi's banks and, tucked beneath the tree line, they provide ultimate waterside privacy in a positively dreamy location.

Camping here is a truly unique experience. Beyond your tent flaps is a scene that changes as much within the hour as most sites do throughout the season. Cobble a morning brew together over the campfire and munch on blackberries as high tide laps beyond your toes and wooden sailing boats sail to and fro across the estuary. Come lunchtime it's become a private beach, the water withdrawing to a narrow channel slithering through the sands while long-legged birds wade along its edges. In fact, the views are of the RSPB's Ynys-hir nature reserve on the opposite shore, so it's no wonder the birdlife is so abundant – sail across at high tide for a closer look.

Landlubbers are just as welcome as those arriving with boat in tow. Head back along the coastal path to where cars are parked and explore the local fishing villages, or better still keep two feet firmly on the ground by venturing into the Snowdonia National Park and walking the ridges towards the north east. The views reveal a vast vista of the estuary below, though don't expect to see the campsite. Tucked in their perfectly secluded location, your tents really are a camping cubbyhole in the wild.

COOL FACTOR As close as you can get to wild camping without having to worry about trespassing laws.

WHO'S IN Tents, families, groups, dogs – yes. Campervans, caravans and motorhomes – no.

ON SITE No vehicle access to the tent pitches, but the site provides a wheelbarrow for carrying your kit and it's only a 100m walk. Toilets and showers are in an ablutions building near the car-parking area. Firewood for sale (by the bag or wheelbarrow-load) and small campfires are permitted. All 3 pitches have outstanding sea views (they're practically in the sea) and, when the tide is out, there is a beach. The Boy John, a converted fishing vessel, is available for groups to use as a communal space or accommodation. It features a sleeping cabin (sleeps 2), piano, log-burning stove, furniture and access to the top deck to enjoy the views.

OFF SITE Go boating on the estuary from the boatyard. If you need a little tuition, try Dyfi Yacht Club (01654 767607) in Aberdyfi (3 miles), a charming, colourful fishing village with a few good eateries and a big sandy beach. The drive takes less than 5 minutes but if the tide is a long way out you can walk, for around an hour, along the sands. It's a 10-minute drive to Machynlleth, a larger market town with independent shops. A little further on the same road is the Centre for Alternative Technology (01654 705950), an interesting place to visit if you're remotely interested in eco-conscious living.

FOOD & DRINK Forage the trees around the camping pitches or get out your fishing rod and try to reel in your own dinner. If you're after something a little more speedy, the local village of Aberdyfi has a range of good eateries specialising in Welsh cuisine, fish and seafood – try the pubby Dovey Inn (01654 767332) overlooking the harbour.

GETTING THERE Take the A493 from Machynlleth for about 6 miles and, after a sharp right then left-hand turn, the entrance to Smuggler's Cove is on the left. There is parking as you enter, then walk under the railway to the estuaryside where you will find the boatyard and camping.

OPEN April–November.

THE DAMAGE A tent and 2 people £15, then £5 per additional person. The Boy John (sleeps 2) from £50 per night.

Hill Fort Tipis

Penparc, Pencaer, Goodwick, Dyfed, Pembrokeshire SA64 0JQ   07415 899342   hillfort-tipis.co.uk

Hill Fort Tipis was created by affable local land owner John, who was born and bred in the farmhouse in this quite incredible corner of Pembrokeshire. John really is the loveliest of owners, an unassuming guy who just wants people to enjoy their time here. Never fear, though; if you don't want chat, he won't force it upon you. And the site? Well, unassuming it definitely is not; instead it is quite simply staggering. You really are camping on top of the world, with the Pembrokeshire coastline unfurling beneath you, like a rolled out carpet.

This immense, panoramic view almost defies description (good job we have some nice photos just over the page!). To put it into perspective, anyone who knows North Pembrokeshire knows that the Strumble Head lighthouse rises from the coastline like an imposing beacon. But, overlooking it from one of Hill Fort's craggy outcrops, Strumble looks like the tiniest, least significant dot in the landscape.

Ironically, the campsite no longer rents out tipis and, while the rest of its name was inspired by the remains of an Iron Age fort on the side of the mountain, it could just as easily be called 'camping in the clouds', for that is about as high as it feels. We often write about a place's sense of space in our guidebooks, but this takes space and freedom to another level. Buzzards and kestrels fly overhead while dolphins can be spotted (with binoculars) from your elevated vantage point. Rabbits and badgers burrow among the gorse. Kids clamber up to the cave in the rocks. The perfect place, then, to contemplate life and all that it has to offer.

COOL FACTOR High pitches with incredible views for the fortunate few that bag a pitch.

WHO'S IN Tents, campervans, dogs (on leads) – yes. Large groups are allowed, but you should contact the site first.

ON SITE 11 camping pitches, each with its own firepit and BBQ, plus 4 yurts available for rent. An old horse lorry houses 2 showers, 2 toilets, a kitchen sink and a communal chill-out area. No electrical hook-ups.

OFF SITE The nearest beaches are the pebbly bays of Abermawr (with its petrified forest, viewable on low spring tides) and Aberbach. Seal lovers can drop down the mountain to Pwllderi, to see pups being born in season. The popular sandy stretches of Whitesands and Newport are within 30 minutes' drive. The area is also a birdwatchers' paradise. Sit in the gorse and listen to the warblers or visit nearby Skomer Island (01646 603110). For the more adventurous, there is coasteering, kayaking and surfing at Preseli (01348 837709).

FOOD & DRINK If you're up for a simple and satisfying meal, such as beer-battered fish and hand-cut Pembrokeshire potato chips, visit The Shed (01348 831518) at Porthgain. The nearby Druidstone Hotel and Restaurant (01437 781221) has been in the Good Food Guide consistently since 1974 and serves delicious homemade food to suit all tastes.

GETTING THERE Take the A40 from Fishguard and drive into Goodwick, then left up Goodwick Hill. Continue on to Heol Penlan Road. Stay on this for 4 miles, passing 2 signs to Strumble Head on the right. After the second, you'll come to a white chapel on your right. Take the next right, signed Hill Fort. Drive up the track and through the gate marked Penparc.

OPEN April–September.

THE DAMAGE Adults from £7.50, children (5–15yrs) from £5; under-5s free. Campervans from £18 per night. Yurts from £75 per night. Plus an initial Greener Camping Club membership fee of £10 per party.

Celtic Camping

Pwll Caerog Farm, Berea, St Davids, Pembrokeshire SA62 6DG   01348 837405   celtic-camping.co.uk

This campsite will have you dancing a little jig of joy as soon as you've stepped foot on its delightful ground. Nuzzling the shores of the Irish Sea, the gaping National Trust land on which the farm and campsite reside offers knock-out views along the coast as well as direct access to the Pembrokeshire Coast Path and a sheltered swimming cove.

Owner Ian is a softly spoken guy who greets campers with warmth and ease. He and his wife Judy opened the site back in 1992 with just a tiny green corner of grass for campers. Since then he's added a flat terrace with electrical hook-ups, situated even closer to the coast, for families. And, because two is never a crowd, a third field – huge, undulating and guarded by a magnificent army of hawthorn bushes – has also been cleared for camping. The farm's evolution didn't stop there; its diminishing outbuildings have also been transformed into an impressive facilities block, while barns have become year-round holiday accommodation, activity and dining spaces, or cosy, ivy-clad bunk houses. The camping meadows have almost become a footnote to the rest of the farm's great holiday offerings, albeit the sort of footnote that you'll instantly remember and will return to again and again and again.

Testament to the site's allure are the tales of grumpy teenagers who arrive in a sulk at the lack of mobile-phone signal but who, after a week of outdoor activities, campfires and barbecues, become tearful when it comes to going home. One or two *Cool Camping* authors may even confess to having felt the same way on packing up their tents…

COOL FACTOR Simple meadows converted into a camping haven, situated on prime National Trust-owned land.

WHO'S IN Tents, campervans, caravans, dogs, groups... the lot!

ON SITE 3 camping fields, with something to suit everyone: the flat family field has electrical hook-ups while the third field has plenty of space for groups. Campfires off the ground: firepits can be borrowed. 2 wash-blocks with showers, loos and sinks (including family and disabled-access rooms). Barn with covered picnic benches and washing-up sinks. Drying room. Bunkhouse accommodation also available onsite.

OFF SITE The pebble beach is a 10-minute walk away – just off the coast path. It's small but has rock pools and is good for swimming. Or ramble along the Pembrokeshire Coastal Path for just over 30 minutes towards Abereiddi's famous Blue Lagoon. Don wetsuits, buoyancy aids and helmets to fling yourselves off the cliffs there and shoot down waterfalls: Celtic Quest Coasteering (01348 837337), recently awarded Best Visitor Experience in Wales by the national tourist board, are based in Abereiddi and will take you out for around 2½ hours.

FOOD & DRINK You can pre-order breakfast (featuring the farm's own sausages and bacon), packed lunches and evening meals (when available). Or follow the coastal path to the famous Sloop Inn (01348 831449) at Porthgain harbour.

GETTING THERE Take the A487 into St Davids and head north out of the city on Nun Street. Take the first left (before the rugby club) and continue along the road for 3½ miles, passing Pembrokeshire Sheepdogs and the nursery. Celtic Camping is on the left, down a farm track.

PUBLIC TRANSPORT Take a train to Haverfordwest, then the Puffin Shuttle (400) to St Davids, from where the Strumble Shuttle (404) drops you near the site on request.

OPEN All year.

THE DAMAGE Adults £10, children (5–15yrs) £5, under-5s free. Electrical hook-ups £5. Bunkhouse bed £24 per person.

Dunes at Whitesands

Craig-Y-Mor, Whitesands Bay, St Davids, Pembrokeshire SA6 26PT   01437 720431   dunesatwhitesands.co.uk

On a sunny day, Whitesands fully justifies its reputation as one of the UK's finest beaches. Famed for its sunsets, when the fiery reflections only accentuate the golden colour of the sand, and renowned as one of the top surf spots in Pembrokeshire, it offers ample space for families and a convenient sliding scale of surfing difficulty – the experienced will find the best waves off the headland on the right of the beach, while novices can stick to the more gentle breakers on the left.

Set back from the sands and just beyond the sea-front golf course, 'Dunes' is an ideal, low-key camping meadow in which to base your Whitesands break. There are just 10 camping pitches on offer, hewn into heathery thicket and grasslands, each with its own picnic table, firepit and 'en-pitch' loo. They're all overlooked by the rare breed balwen sheep that graze the adjacent meadow, and campers can try their hand herding with the owner's working sheep dog, Rhian. The place has a thoroughly laid-back feel, with a basic wooden structure housing the washing-up sinks, two showers in simple cabins and a semi-wilderness of meadow that will appeal to parents who don't mind their children getting grass stains on their knees and molten marshmallows stuck in their woolly jumpers.

It's just over a mile to the smallest city in Britain, where you can explore the cathedral that gives St Davids its name and duck in and out of the various cafés and galleries. Or just stay on the coast and hop from beach to beach and bay to bay. There are plenty to choose from!

COOL FACTOR Surfboards to borrow, campfires permitted and simple, homespun facilities.

WHO'S IN Tents – yes. Motorhomes, caravans, dogs – no.

ON SITE 10 large pitches (2 with electrical hook-ups); each has a firepit, picnic table and en-suite waterless loo. A free bag of logs is provided to get you started. 2 unisex showers. A wooden structure houses washing-up facilities, a fridge/freezer (ice packs available for use) and charging points for your phone. Kayaks, surfboards and beach gear for all to use.

OFF SITE Blue Flag, surfer-friendly Whitesands Beach is a 10-minute walk away, skirting around St Davids City Golf Course (07527 004015) to get there. You can take boards from the campsite and throw yourselves into the waves or simply enjoy a little sandcastle building. It's 1½ miles into St Davids itself. Famed for being Britain's smallest city, it is really little more than a village. But it's one of the most characterful villages in the country and very much characterised by its Celtic heritage. Visit the cathedral (01437 720202) and the bishop's palace (01443 336000) and explore the many galleries.

FOOD & DRINK Whitesands Beach has a decent café. For everything else, St Davids is the place; try The Farmers Arms (01437 721666) and The Bishops (01437 720422) for traditional pub fare.

GETTING THERE At Cross Square in St Davids take the A487 (Nun St) and, after 800m, turn left on to the B4583, following signs to Whitesands. After 100m turn left, staying on the B4583. After 1 mile, just after the Craig-Y-Mor B&B sign, turn left at the crossroads. The site is on the left, by the golf club.

PUBLIC TRANSPORT From St Davids the Strumble Shuttle (404) stops 100m from the site entrance.

OPEN May–September.

THE DAMAGE A pitch and 2 people £260 per week. Extra adults £7.50, children (5–16yrs) £3.80; under-5s free. Plus an initial Greener Camping Club membership of £10 per party.

Porthclais Farm

Porthclais, St Davids, Pembrokeshire SA62 6RR   01437 720616   porthclais-farm-campsite.co.uk

On arrival at Porthclais Farm, you're greeted by a five-day weather forecast. This is indicative of the outdoors life that you can lead here – as well as a helpful and informative approach by the owners. They know that people come here to enjoy everything that the Pembrokeshire coastline has to offer – from walking the coastal path, surfing, sailing, fishing and rock pooling to generally pottering around the coastline. The lower fields have only a gorse hedge between you and the coastal path and the pretty harbour of Porthclais just at the bottom of the cliffs. Depending on your outdoor pursuits you could easily ditch the car for the duration of your stay as the cathedral city of St Davids is only a 15-minute walk away – either back up the lane or, for a slightly longer route with a view, along the coastal path.

This site has a lovely relaxed attitude – from where you pitch, to what you pitch. In high season the site is a lively mix of family frame tents, one-person pop-ups, tipis, bell tents and volleyball/tennis nets. The only real rule is to set up camp 20ft away from strangers and 10ft between friends, but that's just a bit of good old common sense. The ablutions facilities are very good, but if you're camping in one of the lower fields and don't want to get caught short, you may prefer to bring your own toilet tent, which is free of charge. And there are no electric hook-ups but you're also welcome to bring your own generator or solar panels. So, all in all, a pretty perfect place to pitch.

COOL FACTOR A big but intimate site with 180-degree views.

WHO'S IN Tents, caravans, campervans, groups, dogs – yes.

ON SITE 5 fields covering 24 acres for tents (dogs not permitted in 1 of these) and 1 field of 5 acres for caravans and campervans. 2 shower/toilet blocks. For women 9 toilets, 6 showers; for men 6 toilets, 6 urinals, 4 showers. 8 outdoor covered washing-up sinks and wetsuit-washing tub. Recycling bins galore. No campfires, but BBQ stands can be hired for a one-off fee of £1. Phone-charging £1. Freezer pack loan 20p.

OFF SITE Hop on the coastal footpath at the bottom of the camping meadows and stroll the ½ mile to Porthclais Harbour. This naturally sheltered cove was once the cargo port for St Davids. Its wall, restored by the National Trust, dates from the 12th or 13th century and the harbour is still used today by fishing and leisure boats. In the opposite direction, it's a similar sort of stroll to St Non's chapel – where St Non gave birth to St David. Water from the well apparently has healing properties and, whether you believe this or not, being surrounded by a landscape and seascape like this can only be good for body and mind.

FOOD & DRINK The campsite shop sells daily fresh essentials, including milk, bacon and Welsh cakes. St Davids has everything else you might need, including a WI-run market on Thursdays, and pubs and cafés to suit all tastes and budgets, from the friendly Farmer's Arms (01437 721666) to the more upmarket Cwtch (01437 720491) restaurant.

GETTING THERE At St Davids' square, pass the chemist (left), head down Goat Street and stay on this road for 2 miles. Look out for Porthclais Farm on your left, before the harbour.

PUBLIC TRANSPORT Take a train to Haverfordwest or Fishguard and then the Richards Brothers bus to St Davids. The 'Celtic Coaster' buses run via St Davids and will stop on request at Porthclais Campsite between June and September. The Celtic Coaster also stops in Porthclais harbour.

OPEN Easter–end of October.

THE DAMAGE Adults £7, children (5–12yrs) £3, under-5s free. Caravans and campervans £14–£21 a night for 2 people.

Shortlands Farm

Druidston, Haverfordwest, Pembrokeshire SA62 3NE   01437 781234   shortlandsfarm.co.uk

In a region with no shortage of stunning views, the panoramic vistas over St Brides Bay enjoyed from Shortlands Farm are really quite spectacular. The Ledwith family's traditional 29-acre dairy farm at Druidston is a breathtaking, back-to-basics site that makes the ideal camp for those exploring this unspoiled fringe of West Wales. There's a refreshingly laid–back feel to the site – pitches are informal, with campers free to set up camp wherever they please. Perched atop the cliffside, exposed to the elements, there's no better place to watch the sun descend over the Irish Sea.

Distant enough from St Davids to avoid the crowds, with secluded Druidston Haven just 10 minutes away, Shortlands is also well located for the Pembrokeshire Coastal Path – accessible from a bridleway at the bottom of the farm. From your tent you can wander across, hop on the trail and stroll down the slope to a large, tidal beach, or walk the two-and a-half miles south to Broad Haven and Little Haven, where there are further beaches and a clutch of pubs and cafés.

All in all, Shortlands Farm is the perfect base for exploring this unspoiled stretch of coast, and, as any beleaguered rambler can attest, Shortland's hosts' hospitality knows no bounds, from complimentary use of the fridge/freezer to a lend of brazier for campfires. Kate and family are happy to help and have expert knowledge of the best local attractions. Not that you need go anywhere: with the best views for miles, Shortlands Farm is a place you'll want to stick around.

COOL FACTOR A divine Druidston dairy farm that's kindly set aside the best fields for traditional tent campers.

WHO'S IN Tents, small campervans, groups and dogs – yes. They also have a separate Caravan & Motorhome Club site for touring caravans and motorhomes.

ON SITE No allocated pitches – campers can choose their own spot. Wash-block with 3 toilets, 3 hot showers, 2 sinks, a babychanging unit and a large sink outside for washing-up. Fires are allowed but must be off the grass. Limited number of firepits available to borrow (deposit required) and logs for sale.

OFF SITE The Pembrokeshire Coastal Path is 5 minutes from the farm. Druidston Haven is the nearest of many beaches, just a 10–15-minute stroll away. The medieval ruins and seaside charm of St Davids – Britain's smallest city (see p.156) – is a 25-minute drive away.

FOOD & DRINK For fish and chips, The Shed (01348 831518) in Porthgain takes some beating. The Swan Inn (01437 781880) is the pick of the pubs, with a great line in inventive seafood dishes. The Druidstone Hotel (01437 781221) restaurant boasts a decent menu of homecooked dishes and some enviable views overlooking St Brides Bay, plus a bar that's so popular they sometimes have to limit numbers in summer. For supplies, the nearest shop is in Broad Haven – 5 minutes by car or a 40-minute walk along the coastal path.

GETTING THERE From Haverfordwest, take the A487 towards St Davids. Turn left at Simpson Cross (signed Nolton Haven). Go straight over the small crossroads, then turn right into the no through road between a red telephone box and a cream cottage. Go all the way to the end.

PUBLIC TRANSPORT Train to Haverfordwest, then local bus to Newgale, and Puffin Shuttle bus to the end of the farm lane.

OPEN All year.

THE DAMAGE £8 per person per night, under-3s are free.

Walton West Campsite

Lower Foxhill, Walton West, Little Haven, Pembrokeshire SA62 3UA   07980 622673   pembrokeshirecampsite.com

On the stillest of still nights at Walton West Campsite in Pembrokeshire you can hear the waves crashing along the coast. It's less than a mile to the beach (less than a mile to two beaches, in fact) but all the same the soft crunch of water tumbling in upon itself is usually lost beneath a gentle chorus of other sounds. Campfires crackle, marshmallows bubble, wildlife rustles among the bushes and at dusk the resident barn owl can sometimes be heard. They are the sounds of traditional, no-frills camping. And for folks like us heading to the coast, they are exactly what we're looking for.

Set in an organic meadow, where short camping lawns have been mown into irregular aprons of longer wild grass, Walton West Campsite is a simple, small campsite with four flush toilets, two hot showers and a couple of washing-up sinks, but very little else besides. There are no electrical hook-ups – though small campervans are still welcome – and there's no shop, café or playground. The entertainment here is more about having space, peace, being surrounded by nature and with a cracking beach within easy reach.

Little Haven is the closest – a picturesque fishing village with plenty of facilities (car parking, toilets, etc.) and quaint village pubs nestled into a sheltered valley that opens up on to a beautiful golden beach. The sandy bay is dotted with rock pools and spectacular craggy formations to the sides, while there's easy access on to the beach itself – ideal for families with young children, it also offers safe swimming and surfing for all ages and abilities. Once around

the headland, the beach actually stretches much further, linking up with neighbouring Broad Haven. It's here that you can hire water sports equipment to make the most of the surf, or retreat back on to the land to snake your way dreamily along the Pembrokeshire Coastal Path.

At night the skies remain wonderfully dark. The campsite is within the boundaries of Pembrokeshire Coast National Park and not only does this mean spectacular scenery and ample wildlife but also no urban glow once the sun sinks behind the sea. Dusk means putting another log on the fire, wrapping up in a blanket and admiring the spectacular starlit skies. The unblemished views echo the Walton West ethos – that interference and manmade luxuries aren't the way to enjoy nature, and that just leaving things alone works much better. Certainly, aside from a few basic facilities and the occasional trim of the grass, Walton West Campsite been left nicely alone for campers to enjoy. And, at the end of the day, isn't that what camping is all about?

COOL FACTOR A peaceful old-fashioned campsite within strolling distance of the coast.

WHO'S IN Tents, smallish campervans, dogs (on a lead; max 2) – yes. Caravans, large groups wanting to party – no.

ON SITE 15 designated grass pitches. No electrical hook-ups. Basic but clean toilet facilities: 4 flushing toilets, 2 electric showers (£1), 6 fridge/freezers, 2 washing-up sinks with cold water and 2 fresh water taps in the field. Chemical disposal for caravans. Campfires allowed – moveable firepits available free of charge with bagged logs and kindling for sale.

OFF SITE There are 2 stunning beaches less than a mile from the campsite – Little Haven and Broad Haven – about a 15-minute walk away along country lanes, or a couple of minutes' drive to either of the beaches' carparks. Both are excellent spots, with rock pools for kids and great surf for those heading on to the water. Try the Haven Sport Shop (01437 781354) in Broad Haven for kayaks, surfboards and paddleboard hire.

FOOD & DRINK Broad Haven's village shop has everything you need, along with 2 good local cafés – The Ocean (01437 781882) and Seaview Café (the latter serving excellent fish and chips). For a pint or tasty pub grub, try The Castle Inn (01437 781445) or St Brides Inn (01437 781266) in Little Haven. Springfield Farm sells fresh, homegrown produce a few minutes' walk from the campsite (including free-range eggs, salads, tomatoes and Pembrokeshire potatoes) and St Davids hosts a local farmers' market on Thursdays. There's also an excellent market in Haverfordwest on Fridays.

GETTING THERE From Haverfordwest take the B4341 towards Broad Haven. Before you reach Broad Haven, pass the Broadway garage on your right and look out for the next left (on a sharp bend), signed to Little Haven. Take this and, when you reach the bottom of the hill (on the bend), you'll spot the campsite on the left.

PUBLIC TRANSPORT The Puffin Shuttle Bus along the coast drops off at nearby Little Haven and Broad Haven.

OPEN March–September.

THE DAMAGE Adults £10–£12, children (4-15yrs) £6–£8; under-4s free. Dogs £2 per night.

Gupton Farm

Freshwater West, Pembrokeshire SA71 5HW   01646 661640   nationaltrust.org.uk/gupton-farm

Freshwater West may be one of the top surfing spots on the Pembrokeshire coast, and indeed one of the best surfing spots in the country, but for most the miles of coastline that front Gupton Farm and its new National Trust campsite are better known simply for the spectacular sea views. This is a place where the Atlantic makes landfall in a marriage of cliffs, rocks and some of the UK's best beaches. How nice that you can camp just a short walk from it all!

Newly opened in 2017 and with fresh new facilities to boot – showers, toilets, a wet-weather barn and more – Gupton Farm Campsite is a fantastic spot for family tent camping that's been built with sympathy for the old farm surroundings. There's nothing too flashy here and facilities have been tastefully constructed within the old farm barns. Likewise, restricting the meadow to tents and small campervans only ensures the site has a traditional and laid-back ambience, with space for kite-flying and for kids to play ball games. You won't find a static caravan spoiling your view.

It's a short walk down to the beach following a grassy farm track that leads you first into the expansive sand dune system that backs the mile-long sands. Even as you approach the beach you can hear the waves crashing along the bay. It's no surprise, then, that the Welsh National Surfing Championships have been held here several times. There are strong currents at work, though, so it pays to be very careful when you swim, and a lifeguard service is provided during the busier summer months.

Elsewhere, the pamphlets and tourist information provided in the wet weather barn are quick to point you, unsurprisingly, to other National Trust-owned sites, including Stackpole Estate, five miles to the east, where woods, walled gardens and ancient stone circles are waiting to be discovered, along with a pleasant walk to beautiful Barafundle Bay. You can also take shelter in the ivy-clad Olde Worlde Café in Bosherston, a simple place but with everything you need – including monster-sized sandwiches and a good old cup of tea.

COOL FACTOR National Trust-owned meadows within strolling distance of the nation's (frequently voted) best beach.

WHO'S IN Tents, campervans, dogs (on a lead), groups – yes. Caravans, motorhomes – no.

ON SITE 50 grass pitches, 5 electric pitches and 1 hardstanding. No campfires but raised BBQs okay. Rustic but well-kept facilities, including a toilet and shower block, a wet-weather barn and communal areas. Farmhouse accommodation also available. The peninsula is shared with the Ministry of Defence, who use the Castlemartin Range for military training. On rare occasions, live firing can be heard.

OFF SITE Film buffs will recognise Freshwater West from *Harry Potter and the Deathly Hallows* and Ridley Scott's version of *Robin Hood,* among other films. Follow the track from the campsite straight down to the sands – a short stroll, even with full bodyboard, bucket and spade and crabbing net. There are several other paths from the campsite too, linking up with the main Pembrokeshire Coastal Path. The National Trust's Stackpole Estate (01646 623110) is only a short drive away and campers are given free parking.

FOOD & DRINK For an unpretentious daytime bite try the Olde Worlde Café (01646 661216) in Bosherston – a white-washed house underneath the heaviest coating of ivy you've ever seen. For something quicker, and closer, the award-winning shack, Café Môr (01646 278101), is right by the beach.

GETTING THERE From Pembroke, follow the B4319 to Castlemartin. Continue on the road and the turning to the farm is on the right a mile after the village and before you descend to Freshwater West beach. It's a concealed entrance; look for the National Trust's pink banner.

PUBLIC TRANSPORT Pembroke (6 miles away) is the nearest train station. The Coastal Cruiser bus (387/388) operates daily (May–Sept), stopping at Freshwater West and Castlemartin.

OPEN Early May–end of September.

THE DAMAGE Tents £10, with a hook-up £6. Campervans £16. You also need to be a National Trust member or purchase a camping pass (£10) to stay at Gupton Farm.

Hillend

Llangennith, Gower, Swansea SA3 1JD   01792 386204   hillendcamping.com

At the far western edge of the Gower Peninsula, Rhossili Bay, a spectacular four-mile sweep of sand, spreads wide and flat northwards from Rhossili town to the tiny offshore islet of Burry Holmes. From the elevated vantage point of Worm's Head in Rhossili, it seems to stretch forever, a colossal swathe of surf-kissed beach that you can either access from Rhossili itself or at the other end near the town of Llangennith, where a narrow country road leads to a beach car park and the unassuming surfers' encampment of Hillend.

Occupying some prime real estate behind the grassy dunes, Hillend campsite has had something of a makeover in recent years. After suffering a reputation for all-night parties and boisterous teenage gangs from Swansea, the owners decided to go for a fresh start. They designated two of the four fields as 'family only', began turning away groups of dodgy-looking youths and built a 'posh' family café and one of the finest amenities blocks on any Welsh campsite. The result is a site that offers a more amenable, grown-up experience while successfully retaining its relaxed, surf-dude heritage. Litter-picking in the sand dunes is now much more likely to turn up empty bottles of champagne and vintage wine rather than flagons of cheap cider.

It's a big site, with 275 pitches on 14 acres of level meadowland, but the new-ish shower block can easily cope with the numbers and there's more than enough room for everyone to share the large beach during even the busiest of busy days. Beginners and intermediate surfers will find the conditions at Rhossili Bay perfect, with a combination of the full Atlantic swell and a gently sloping beach producing long waves that can be ridden (with a bit of practice) for more than 100 metres. The Welsh Surfing Federation (01792 386426; wsfsurfschool.co.uk) runs two-hour surfing lessons from their permanent base on the beach, too, from around £25 per person. They've been operating here since the early 1980s and certainly know their stuff.

But the appeal of Hillend is more than just the beach, the surf and the Gower landscape. There's a pull about this part of the peninsula that has a deep and lasting effect on visitors. Maybe it's the wild and remote atmosphere, enhanced by the crashing Atlantic waves, or the ethereal wind stirring up the grassy dunes? Or maybe it's the fact that the rowdy mob and troublemakers have been banished. Whatever the reason, why not try a weekend's camping at Hillend and see if you too succumb to its mystical charms?

COOL FACTOR Surfside location and first-rate facilities.

WHO'S IN Tents, small campervans – yes. Caravans, dogs – no.

ON SITE The shower block has 26 showers plus outside showers for surfers, washing-up and laundry facilities. Nextdoor, Eddy's Bistro (usually open 8am–8pm) serves inexpensive snacks and meals, and a shop sells camping essentials, groceries and beach paraphernalia. 8 whole acres of the site are dedicated to family camping and there is a children's play area too.

OFF SITE Walk the ¾-mile back into Llangennith, whose houses are clustered round a village green and the church of St Cenydd – the largest in Gower, founded in the 6th century. According to legend the church was established by St Cenydd but in 986 was destroyed by Vikings and the present, Norman structure dates from the 12th century. There's a good pub (see *Food & Drink*) opposite PJ's Surf Shop (01792 386669), where you can also arrange lessons. From the campsite, walk north-west through the dunes to the Blue Pool (1½ miles away), a rock pool which, in the right sea and sky conditions, takes on a deep blue colour.

FOOD & DRINK A 5-minute drive or 15-minute walk back up the road is The King's Head (01792 386212), popular with surfers for its music, pool tables and affordable pub grub.

GETTING THERE Hillend is just over a mile west of Llangennith. Pick up the B4295 westwards on the Gower and continue all the way until it hits the sea.

PUBLIC TRANSPORT Bus 116 from Swansea goes to Llangennith, from where it's a mile's walk.

OPEN Easter–late October.

THE DAMAGE A pitch and up to 3 people £20–£25. Additional adults £3–£5, children (under 16) £2. The 'no advance booking' policy is a notorious nightmare on summer weekends; best bet is to get there on Thursday night or send someone down early with the tents to reserve and pay for everyone.

Skysea Campsite

Port Eynon, Gower, Swansea SA3 1NN 01792 390795 porteynon.com

The sleepy village of Port Eynon on the Gower Peninsula is dominated by campsites, and static caravans occupy various hillside fields above the town. But help is at hand at Skysea (formerly known as Carreglwyd), which has five camping fields, of which only the two nearest reception are favoured by caravans, with tents having the run of the place beyond.

All in all, it's a well-organised and well-equipped site, with modern showers that are both clean and free, plus a very good onsite launderette and a small shop at reception for the basics. But above all its direct access to the beach makes it a perfect place for young families, with a half-mile crescent of calm, kid-friendly waters and plenty of water sports opportunities. In short, it's family-heaven during summer.

If the sun is a no-show, head the other way out of the campsite, where a maze of paths cover the headland. This land is owned and managed by the National Trust, but it feels wild and untamed, with multiple caves to explore as well as Culver Hole, a mysterious four-storey building secreted into the rocks of the headland. Its origin may have been defensive, but it's probably seen more use as a smugglers' hideout.

Fall Bay is perhaps the most unspoiled beach in the area, while evenings should be spent following the coastal path to Worm's Head and Rhossili. The spectacular five-mile walk showcases the most dramatic stretch of Gower coastline and possibly the best sunset in the UK — proof alone of why Gower was selected as Britain's first official Area of Outstanding Natural Beauty.

COOL FACTOR Static caravan excess gives way to utterly unspoiled coastline.

WHO'S IN Tents, campervans, caravans, dogs (on a lead at all times), families – yes. Big groups, young groups – no.

ON SITE 2 modern amenities blocks with toilets, hot showers, basins, laundry and washing-up facilities. An onsite shop sells groceries and camping accessories. Electrical hook-ups and chemical disposal points. No campfires permitted but BBQs are allowed provided they are raised well off the grass.

OFF SITE Gower Coast Adventures run boat trips from Port Eynon to Worm's Head (07866 250440) – perfect for spotting gannets, guillemots and even puffins. For those after a water-based adrenalin kick, surfboards can be rented and lessons taken at Sam's Surf Shack in Rhossili (01792 350519). Or, for something really different, paragliding off the headland in Rhossili is also hugely popular.

FOOD & DRINK Among places to eat in Port Eynon, the newly refurbished Ship Inn (01792 390204) is chock-full of seafaring décor and serves award-winning Gower Brewery ales. The Smugglers Haunt (01792 391257) does pizzas and pub grub and The Seafarer (01792 380879) decent fish and chips. A 5-mile walk or short bus ride away in Rhossili village, The Worm's Head Hotel (01792 390512) serves regional seafood specials, such as Penclawdd cockles, Burry Port mussels and line-caught Gower sea bass. Make sure you bag a table on the terrace – it's a stunning spot at sunset.

GETTING THERE Take the A4118 from Swansea (signposted Mumbles) and follow it all the way to the end. The entrance to Skysea is just by the beach car park at Port Eynon.

PUBLIC TRANSPORT Regular buses run from Swansea run to Port Eynon, stopping a few yards from the site entrance.

OPEN All year.

THE DAMAGE Pitch and family of 4 from £25. Additional adults £8, children (4–16yrs) £2, under-4s free. Hook-ups £5.

Heritage Coast Campsite

Monknash, Cowbridge, Vale of Glamorgan CF71 7QQ   01656 890399   heritagecoastcampsite.com

The seaside trails of Snowdonia, the Gower and Pembrokeshire need little introduction, but have you heard of the Glamorgan Heritage Coast Path? Starting from Cardiff Bay's regenerated waterfront and spanning 35 miles westwards to the seaside kitsch of Porthcawl, this stretch of Wales' recently opened national trail takes in some of the country's most spectacular scenery. The sweeping sands of Whitmore Bay, the film-famed dunes of Merthyr Mawr, coastal cafés and charming clifftop villages – it's a wonder the area isn't positively overrun. Not that we're complaining. It's all the more reason to set up base at well-placed Heritage Coast Campsite.

Glyn and Philippa George know a thing or two about hospitality. Having run their successful five-star B&B to much acclaim, the Georges decided to share their stunning corner of Monknash with the canvas contingent. Opening up the adjoining brook-side paddock for a 28-day test a couple of years back, the response was so overwhelming that the ever-generous pair realised it would be a shame to keep it to themselves. And so the campsite was born.

This tents-only spot had space for just 30 privileged pitches with uninterrupted views of the undulating Glamorgan hills and the sparkling Bristol Channel (you can almost hear the "oo ar"s from Devon on a clear day). Facilities are second to none, with a brand-new stables block housing immaculately clean ablutions and a fully licensed café. The result is a thoroughly chilled-out, family campsite, with views to savour, a brook to meditate beside and, of course, those undiscovered miles of coastal path to explore.

COOL FACTOR A beautiful family campsite on an undiscovered and underrated stretch of Welsh coastline.

WHO'S IN Tent campers, families, well-behaved dogs – yes. Groups – at the owners' discretion (i.e. no noisey parties).

ON SITE 2 paddocks with space for 30 tents. For minimal impact, facilities are designed to look like stables, housing gents' and ladies' ablutions, with 2 toilets, 2 showers, 2 sinks, hand dryer, plus a hairdryer in the ladies'. Unisex disabled bathroom with babychanging facilities. Utility room with washbasins, freezer, lockers. Fully licensed café and bar (see *Food & Drink*). Disposable BBQs not allowed, but firepits are available and logs sold (though you can't bring your own).

OFF SITE Pick up the Glamorgan Heritage Coast Path and head north to Southerndown and Dunraven Bay – popular with surfers and just about everyone else in summer. Escape the crowds with a visit to the Heritage Coast Centre (01656 880157). Nearby Merthyr Mawr Sand Dunes were the backdrop to the epic *Lawrence of Arabia* and the village's charming thatched cottages still attract the film industry today.

FOOD & DRINK The campsite plays host to the excellent Teddy's Bar & Kitchen, a fully licensed eatery open daily, complete with log-burner for chilly days and local artwork on display. Chow down to a home-cooked breakfast or grab light meals and sandwiches during the day. 300 yards from the site you'll also find the excellent, timbered Plough & Harrow (01656 890209), which offers a fine selection of real ales, decent pub grub and live music on Saturday evenings.

GETTING THERE Follow the dual carriageway to Bridgend; at the 5th roundabout take the St Brides Major turnoff (B4265) and a mile beyond the village, take the right turn to Monknash and follow the signs for the Plough & Harrow; turn right past the pub and continue for 300m.

OPEN March–October.

THE DAMAGE Pitch and 2 people from £16 a night.

WELSH
BREAKFAST
LARGE ROLLS
OR
BAGUETTES
BACON
SAUSAGE
EGG
MU
F

Seaside Campsites in France

For guaranteed good weather, sublime food and seaside campsites with a certain *je ne sais quoi*, it's tough to beat a holiday in France.

Whether it's the reliable weather, the fine wine or the added sense of escapism that comes from struggling with a foreign language and driving on the wrong side of the road, it doesn't take much to convince us to go on holiday to France.

We've travelled thousands of miles, visited hundreds of campsites and eaten far more baguettes than should reasonably be consumed to bring together the best French campsites for coolcamping.com. So, for those of you camping on the continent this summer, we've included a hand-picked selection of our top 10 seaside spots in this printed guidebook too.

And what campsites they are, all set within striking distance of the sparkly sea. And, since this is France, even the most basic campsites seem to abide by certain unwritten rules – there must be a boules pitch, fresh croissant delivery is essential and, no matter what region you settle in, it's bound to have some world-class local cuisine that you can only find at home for five times the price.

So, *mes amis*, brush off your phrasebook, wave *au revoir* to pints of flat beer and head for the blue French yonder. *Bon voyage, bonne chance... et bon appétit*!

Camping Bel Sito

A tarmac trail leads 800 metres through the dunes behind Baubigny beach to Camping Bel Sito, a low-key, 85-pitch campsite that offers refreshment from the big Europarks further along the coast. There's a playground, a ping-pong table and Wi-Fi by reception, but otherwise it has a wonderfully undeveloped feel. Given the proximity of the dunes, pitches are more sandy than grassy, but head to the bottom of the site – where there's a small lake – and the ground's a little firmer. It's a 10-minute drive to Barneville-Carteret, where you can catch a ferry to Guernsey, or stay put and explore the beaches of the gorgeous Cherbourg Peninsula.

Normandy   0033 (0)2 3304 3274
camping-normandie-belsito.com

Camping du Letty

A kilometre from the summer resort of Bénodet in Brittany, the mature trees and abundant hedges at long-established Camping du Letty give a real sense of seclusion. It's easy to forget you're in the biggest tentopolis along this stretch of coast – 25 acres with around 550 pitches plus bars, a disco and a swimming pool with slides and a retractable roof. The campsite abuts Plage de Groasguen, a thin strip of lagoon-side sand at the mouth of the River Odet. Across the water the Dunes Dominiales de Mousterlin block the sea's swell, resulting in a choice between paddling-friendly backwaters on your tent-step or a real beach and bigger waves just a short hike away.

Brittany   0033 (0)2 9857 0469   campingduletty.com

Camping de l'Océan

Long, sandy stretches front the neo-classical centre of France's first beach resort, Soulac-sur-Mer, where bijou boutiques and eateries suit all tastes. Just 300 metres back from Plage de l'Amélie, Camping de l'Océan provides the finest camping area along this stretch of the Côte d'Argent (Silver Coast). Their set-up is exemplary. A snack bar, reception and washrooms are designed to blend in with the surroundings and everything you need is on site. If it's not, just grab a bike and pedal until you find it – the 141-kilometre track following the Médoc coast to Les Landes vindicates the tourist board's claim that Soulac is 'close to everything except boredom'.

Gironde   0033 (0)5 5609 7610   sandaya.fr

Huttopia Côte Sauvage

Tucked among tufts of marram grass and flowering sand-verbena, you couldn't pitch your tent closer to Île de Ré's Basse Benaie beach if you tried. Set 20 metres from the sea, Côte Sauvage campsite and the dunes have become one, with stick beach fencing dividing up different areas and a playground rising from the natural crash mat of the sand. From Basse Benaie you can walk further along the coast to Montamer beach – one of the island's most popular swimming spots at high tide – or hire a bike and follow some of the 100 kilometres of car-free trails that make exploring Île de Ré such a delight.

Île de Ré   0033 (0)4 3764 2235   huttopia.com

Bot-Conan Lodge

With its own private sandy beach, flanked by woods on all sides, Bot-Conan Lodge is a positive paradise for those seeking to retreat from the crowds on the Brittany coast. A dozen family-sized safari lodges ensure this is a rather exclusive site where glamping, rather than camping, is on offer. Each tent maximises on living space with an outdoor kitchen and separate bathroom facilities, while the meadow leading to the beach has ample space for picnicking and games. The port of Concarneau is just across the bay, where a captivating fishing museum chronicles the town's main industry. A visit to the museum is best followed by sampling the seafood al fresco overlooking the harbour.

Brittany   0033 (0)6 1105 1943   botconan.com

Domaine La Yole

This camping behemoth 75 kilometres south-east of Montpellier declares itself not just a campsite but, also, a 'wine resort'. The latter word certainly rings true – the 'aqua area' is vast, with slides, pools and sun loungers galore; there's an adventure park in the trees, mini-golf, bike hire and no fewer than six different ablutions buildings. But the well-shaded pitches are surprisingly spacious and the wine heritage couldn't be more genuine. There have been vineyards here since Roman times and today you can tour the site's vast cellars and taste a sip of the 700,000 litres produced annually. It's a 600-metre walk down Avenue de la Méditerranée to sandy Vendres beach.

Herault   0033 (0)4 6737 3387   campinglayole.com

Panorama du Pyla

Beyond the glitzy west coast resort of Arcachon is Europe's tallest sand dune. From the campsite below, people's matchstick silhouettes can be seen trekking towards the summit of Dune du Pyla, rewarded with sunsets that engulf the Bay of Biscay. The campsite is a busy affair in high summer – a fancy restaurant and ice-cream parlour, two swimming pools, and kids' entertainment create a boisterous atmosphere. The ergonomics work, however, with amenities grouped near the entrance so that the noisier activities precede the quiet among the coniferous trees. Drive into Arcachon for fine dining among the pricey Victorian villas or catch the ferry to laid-back Cap Ferret.

Gironde   0033 (0)5 5622 1044   camping-panorama.com

Le Balcon de la Baie

Set back from the coast but with far-reaching views to Mont St-Michel Bay (and 15km from the world-famous, monastery-topped island that bears the same name) this family-run campsite is well placed for UK ferries. Half an hour's drive from St Malo port, it has less than 40 shrub-divided pitches centred around an irregularly shaped swimming pool. Family essentials are covered – there's a playground, a games room, plus plenty of open space for a game of badminton or pétanque. It's a flat and rather uninspiring walk to the very nearest bit of coast, so drive to the attractions near Mont St-Michel instead or explore St Malo's fascinating old town.

Normandy   0033 (0)2 9980 2295   lebalcondelabaie.com

Camping les Chênes Verts

France's second largest island after Corsica, Île d'Oléron is a place where bicycles reign supreme. From the pine forest in Saint-Trojan-les-Bains to the Chassiron lighthouse on the northern tip, trails cover no fewer than 110 kilometres of the 172-kilometre-squared isle. Directly beside such a trail, wooded Camping les Chênes Verts has about 100 tent pitches and happily rents out bikes to campers as part of its 'get active' ethos. It also boasts a playground, pétanque court, volleyball and table tennis, plus a heated outdoor swimming pool. Beach-wise, it's 50 metres down to the waterside at Passe de l'Ecuissière, a sandy shore that's safe for paddling and increasingly popular for horseriding too.

Île d'Oléron   0033 (0)5 4675 3288   huttopia.com

Les Eucalyptus

Beyond their cute co-operative vineyard, Philippe and Florence Lamon also run a small (40 pitches) farm campsite, where the occasional sound of a tractor is drowned out by the inviting roar of waves on adjacent Moorea Plage, part of St-Tropez's legendary Pampelonne sands. Boutiques selling cool clothes fringe the restaurants at the end of the beach and there's a fine-dining area that wouldn't look out of place in nearby St-Tropez. Even further towards Pampelonne's world-famous Plage de Tahiti, is another, larger campsite with its own on-site supermarket. Perfect for stocking up before retreating to the superior privacy of Les Eucalyptus.

French Riviera   0033 (0)4 9497 1674
campingleseucalyptus.fr

Lochranza

Lochranza, Isle of Arran, North Ayrshire KA27 8HL 01770 830273 arran-campsite.com

Of all the wildly enchanting islands and atolls scattered off the west Scottish mainland, the Isle of Arran is arguably the most magnificently varied of these rocky outcrops. Scythed in half by the subterranean Highland Boundary Fault, this easily navigable 19 mile-long island boasts a remarkable diversity of sea, rock and wild grassland. To the south, undulating countryside and vibrant coastal pockets are offset against the distinctive sills and dykes – remnants of the natural forces that shaped this land. While, to the north, dramatic mountains borne of primordial battles between fire and ice are awash with vibrant Scottish heather.

Nestled within a weather-bitten chunk of the island's northern tip, Lochranza is a fishing village of such picture-postcard perfection, it's almost absurd. Situated on the shores of a small sea loch, the village plays hosts to not only a 13th century castle and cluster of friendly B&Bs, but also the ideally situated and far more rewarding resting place of Lochranza Camping and Caravanning Site.

On a flat clearing, hugged lovingly by the towering sides of the glen, Lochranza is a one of the region's most scenic spots in which to pitch. A scattering of informal grassy spaces provides the perfect place to pop your tent and soak up the views, while a handful of insulated pods offer comfort to visitors travelling light. The site is abuzz with wildlife (including an inquisitive red deer population) making it a favourite with bird watchers and helping it win the Gold Award from Green Tourism in 2017. What's more, the campsite boasts a 9-hole golf course and a whisky distillery moments away. What more could you ask for?

COOL FACTOR Whisky tasting, golf club swinging and bird-spotting fun in a geologically fascinating setting.

WHO'S IN Tents, caravans, campervans, dogs, groups – yes.

ON SITE 60 level pitches (some hardstandings and some with electricity) and 4 camping pods. Showers, toilets, basins and hairdryers. Disabled access washroom. Cooking shelter and launderette with sink, tumble dryer and drying cupboard for walking gear. Covered dish-washing area and campers' room with tourist information, fridges and a microwave. Shop selling camping gas, maps, guide books and golf products. Pay-and-play 9-hole golf course (adults £12; juniors £6; clubs hire £6), plus 2 putting greens, a 9-hole pitch-and-putt and a picnic area.

OFF SITE Walking galore around Arran's varied coast and on the dramatic mountain ridges, including up the beautiful Goatfell. For something lengthy, the Arran Coastal Way takes around a week. Whisky afficionados should head to the Isle of Arran Distillery (01770 830264) to sample some of the island's famous single malt. If cheese is more your thing, pop along to the Arran Cheese Shop (01770 302788) to see the island's second most famous export being waxed with artisan care. The area also boasts the Machrie Moor Stone Circles, Kings Caves and 13th-century Lochranza Castle – the inspiration for one of Tintin's adventures.

FOOD & DRINK Opposite the golf course, you'll find the popular Stags Pavilion restaurant (01770 830600) open in the evenings – it's BYOB. The Sandwich Station (07810 796248) on Lochranza Pier does great snacks and light bites with an excellent local deli. Or enjoy golden eagle spotting in The Isle of Arran Distillery's Casks Café (01770 830264).

GETTING THERE Turn right out of Brodick ferry terminal and head north. Out of Sannox the road climbs over open hillsides then descends into Lochranza. Pass the Isle of Arran Distillery on the left then, shortly after, on the right, look for the Lochranza Golf Course and Campsite sign.

OPEN Late March–end of October.

THE DAMAGE From £18 depending on size of tent (2 adults included). Children (6–16yrs) £4.

Muasdale

Muasdale, Tarbert, Argyll PA29 6XD   01586 421559   muasdale.com

Fancy a challenge? How about heading down a seeming road-to-nowhere in search of Kintyre, a place that truly encapsulates the phrase 'out on a limb'? Getting anywhere near Kintyre can itself be a long and arduous undertaking, involving a route around the shores of both Loch Lomond and Loch Fyne. You can try crossing the two lochs aboard a ferry – it may not be any quicker, but it's more relaxed and even feels a little exotic – or take the recently opened direct route, ferrying all the way across the Firth of Clyde from Ardrossan with dramatic views of the Isle of Arran along the way.

But is Kintyre really worth all that travel time? Well, rest assured that the doubts that may have plagued you along the way (despite all the glorious scenery en route) are bound to evaporate on reaching this very special place. Perching on not-so-towering cliffs that measure just over a metre in height, Muasdale Holiday Park sits directly above the purest white sands. The calm waters that reside in this bay are so sheltered that, despite the campsite's proximity to the water's edge, there's no danger of sharing your sleeping bag with the sea.

The beach itself is exceedingly beautiful and the water warm enough for extended bathing in summer. But what really stole the hearts of the *Cool Camping* team was the view over the water to the islands of Islay and Jura. It wouldn't be out of the question to simply sit here with a good book for a whole week, occasionally glancing around to confirm you've won big in the lottery of life.

Taken over in 2016 by friendly owners Alan and Ailsa McCuaig, the campsite is part of the tiny straggling village of Muasdale, which retains an air of everyday life about it that is yet to be troubled by tourism. The camping area takes up a slither of well-drained, midge-free ground between the main road and the calm sea and, with no more than eight pitches available, it's a rather small affair. The official *Cool Camping* inspection took place over the school holidays, but the place wasn't full, nor did the road prove noisy at night, even though we slept right next to it.

Should you finish your book, hole your canoe, break your bucket and spade or lose your Speedos, it's worth popping your derrière on to a bike saddle, as the mainly flat road on the western side of Kintyre is made for two-wheelers. The ferry to the small island of Gigha is a four-mile pedal, or you could present your thighs with a real challenge and cycle the amazingly scenic road on the eastern side of the peninsula. Surf dudes and chicks can find some serious waves at Machrihanish Bay, or you could take a ferry ride to the island of Islay to the west, where the distilleries produce some of the finest malts in the world. If you do take your bike over, stick to the east of the island and enjoy the impressive sights of nearby Jura as you pedal.

On the other hand, that might be one challenge too many, so maybe just sit back, relax and open another book.

COOL FACTOR Small, friendly and remarkably midge-free beachside site miles from anywhere remotely touristy. Great for cyclists and canoeists.

WHO'S IN Tents, campervans, caravans, dogs – yes. Motorhome or caravan set-ups over 7m long – no.

ON SITE 8 pitches. 1 wooden pod with 2 single beds and 1 log cabin with a hot tub also available. Well-maintained toilets and hot showers. Firepits available to use and fire-starting kits available. BBQs permitted but must be raised off the grass. Free Wi-Fi. Recycling and charging facilities. Boat launching.

OFF SITE The joy of this place is the utter seclusion. But that does leave you hard pressed for nearby attractions. Enjoy a good book, explore the sandy beach, try a spot of fishing or launch a boat. Those with canoes and bikes love the place. Stretching from Tarbert at the north end of the peninsula to Dunaverty in the south, the way-marked Kintyre Way footpath is a popular walking route and connects communities across the peninsula.

FOOD & DRINK The Argyll Hotel (01583 421212) at Bellochantuy, 5 miles south, is famous for being sprayed with machine-gun bullets by an aircraft just after the outbreak of the Second World War – it turned out to be an RAF plane testing its weaponry. It should be safe now, though, and has a good selection of food. For more choice, head into Campbeltown where, among the eatieres, there are also no fewer than 3 different distilleries.

GETTING THERE Take the A82 from Glasgow, then the A83 through Inveraray, Lochgilphead and Tarbert. Muasdale is 22 miles south of Tarbert, alongside the A83. Alternatively, use the ferry from Ardrossan to Campbeltown then pick up the A83 and follow for 14 miles to Muasdale. The campsite is ¼ mile after you enter the village and tough to miss.

PUBLIC TRANSPORT A regular bus service from Glasgow passes the site, but it does take 4 hours! Traveline (08712 002233; travelinescotland.com) has details of times and stops.

OPEN April–end of September.

THE DAMAGE Pitch and 2 people from £15 per night.

Port Bàn

Port Bàn Holiday Park, Kilberry, Tarbert, Argyll PA29 6YD   01880 770224   portban.com

Ever felt like you've camped at the edge of the earth? No? Then come to Port Bàn. This tiny community near Kilberry on the unspoiled Knapdale Peninsula may look like the last stop in Scotland but, of course, that's the attraction. The sheer beauty of this primitive landscape, coupled with its rich diversity of wildlife, makes Port Bàn a fascinating retreat for any intrepid camper.

On a practical level, the site has all the essentials – ablutionary facilities are clean, orderly and more than adequate – while traditional campers should be aware that Port Bàn also caters for caravans and motorhomes. However, big wagon drivers and canvas campers are in separate fields, all enjoying flat, well-maintained pitches and truly idyllic views across the North Atlantic to Islay and Jura islands (book early for the best shoreside spots).

Above all else, the place has a real sense of the epic. Separated for centuries from the rest of Scotland by lochs and mountains that define the region, the Knapdale Peninsula remains secluded and sparsely populated. For lovers of history, there's an exceptional range of ancient sites nearby, including monuments, castles and historic houses where Scotland's turbulent past, clan heritage and rich history will delight.

Yet, despite the attractions, peaceful atmosphere, approachable owners and never-ending list of onsite facilities, the real highlight of Port Bàn has to be its jaw-dropping sunsets. There is little point trying to describe it; you really must experience it for yourself. Suffice to say, nothing soothes the urban soul quite like viewing its full-colour glory from your beach-based campfire.

COOL FACTOR Glorious isolation, heaps of family-friendly facilities and memorable sunsets.

WHO'S IN Tents, caravans, motorhomes and dogs – yes.

ON SITE 30 pitches with electric hook-ups. Facilities – showers, toilets and large sinks – are clean and more than adequate, with disabled access too. Launderette and phone box. Shop, café, restaurant and daytime lounge. Children's playground, games hall with pool and table tennis, tennis, crazy golf, volleyball and a beach. Campfires permitted on the beach. Bikes for hire.

OFF SITE The campsite is well placed on the Sustrans Cycle Route 78 (Campbeltown–Oban) and a local network of Forestry Commission roads is ideal for mountain bikes and walkers. Visit the beavers in the Scottish Beaver Trial, a project to introduce beavers back into Scotland (after 400 years of extinction in the UK). There's also the Kilmartin House Museum (01546 510278) of local archeology. The ancient church nextdoor is an interesting artefact in itself, too.

FOOD & DRINK The onsite Seaview Café (closed on Sunday) serves coffee, cakes, simple meals and takeaways, while the famous Kilberry Inn (01880 770223), one of Scotland's leading seafood restaurants, is within walking distance. Elsewhere, you're spoiled for choice in Tarbert, 15 miles away.

GETTING THERE Take the M8 west, leaving at signs for Erskine Bridge. Go over the bridge and head towards the A82 (to Campbeltown). Head up the side of Loch Lomond to Tarbet and the road becomes the A83. Continue on to Lochgilphead, where you turn left to Campbeltown. Continue through Ardrishaig, then a right turn (to Kilberry) takes you to the single track B8024 road. A further 15 miles and Port Bàn is signposted on the right.

OPEN April–October.

THE DAMAGE Pitch and 2 people from £22. Extra adults £4; children (6–15yrs) £2, under-6s free. Dogs £2.

Ardnamurchan

Ormsaigberg, Kilchoan, Acharacle, Argyll PH36 4LL   01972 510766   ardnamurchanstudycentre.co.uk

Ancient Celtic traditions say that over the western sea, beyond the edge of any map, lies the afterlife. Sitting at Ardnamurchan campsite it's certainly easy to believe, as you watch the sun torch the ocean between the scattered Hebrides, that you're as close as you can get to Heaven on Earth.

The site clings to the coast just a few miles from the tip of a rocky finger of land that's as far west as Britain goes. You approach it (slowly) via a ferry and a sinuous single-track road that hems in the crumpled and craggy landscape and makes getting here an escapade in itself. The site is situated to the west of the beautiful village of Kilchoan, on a small south-facing croft that has stunning views down the Sound of Mull to Morven and Mull. This far-flung location makes it the most westerly campsite on the British mainland.

Remarkably, it is the brainchild of one man, Trevor Potts, who has turned an old croft into this Elysian camping field. The site may seem rough-and-ready at first glance, a slice of wild hillside only just tamed, but as you settle in you'll appreciate just how much Trevor has transformed the place. Every pitch has been cut from the slope and levelled, and he's recently vanquished a field of seven-foot-high bracken to open up a new camping area. Trevor also built the toilet block with recycled materials, and crafted a replica of Shackleton's remarkable little boat next door. There is nothing particularly fancy or arty about it all, but Trevor did the lot himself, and everything fits in neatly with the surroundings.

Pitches range from neat nooks with hook-ups near the wash-block to wilder spots closer to the shore. If you camp right at the bottom of the slope you will be lulled to sleep by the wash of wave on rock. The foreshore is rough, rocky and just right for a scramble. You can catch creatures in the rockpools, throw stones at the waves or simply watch the ferries weaving their way along to nearby islands. The facilities are humble and homely with surprisingly powerful showers. Flowers add a burst of colour to the whitewashed walls, and there can't be many wash-blocks that have their very own salvaged whale skeleton.

So, what else does the Ardnamurchan Peninsula have to tempt campers? Well, some of the loveliest beaches on the planet can be found around the campsite's edges. Just a few miles away are the particularly glorious sands of Sanna, which are lapped by turquoise waters. The drive there takes you through a jagged, almost extra-terrestrial landscape of steep cliffs and snaggle-toothed ridges. If you'd visited 55 million years ago you'd have witnessed an epic volcanic spectacle. Fastforward through a few Ice-Age scourings and today you see a rocky ring more than three miles across, the remnant of a volcano quite unlike any other in Britain. Further on around the coast, another age of history was brought back to life at Swordle Bay when, in 2011, archaeologists unearthed a rare Viking burial boat. Although you can't see much more now than the mound of stones that marks the spot, you can watch an occasional summer recreation of the boat's burial.

After a day's exploring and an evening watching yet another sunset, it's not hard to understand why people have been coming here for thousands of years.

COOL FACTOR The view, the wildlife (otters, pine martens, sea eagles and golden eagles), the beaches... and the beautiful journey to get here.

WHO'S IN Tents, campervans, groups, dogs – yes. Large motorhomes, caravans – no.

ON SITE Basic and quaintly ramshackle, with toilets, showers, laundry and dish-washing facilities. 20 pitches and 4 campervan hook-ups, 2 loos and 2 free, powerful showers. You can also hire 1 of 2 caravans and a bothy. Washing-up area with fridge. Internet access. No campfires.

OFF SITE Join campsite owner Trevor on one of his guided walks or attend one of his lectures on local, as well as Antarctic, geology and wildlife. Stroll on the sandy beach at Sanna, reached by passing through an extraordinary volcanic landscape. Visit the lighthouse at Ardnamurchan Point, the most westerly part of the British mainland, and climb the tower (01972 510210). Nearby Ben Hiant is a terrific wee mountain with superb views. You can also pop over to Tobermory on Mull by ferry from Kilchoan (0800 066 5000).

FOOD & DRINK There's a fine and fun coffee shop in an old stable at the Ardnamurchan Lighthouse. Bar meals and finer evening dining are on offer at The Kilchoan House Hotel (01972 510200), 1½ miles away. Guests are also encouraged to bring their own instruments along to create impromptu music in the public bar. There's also good food available at The Sonachan Hotel (01972 510211) on the way to the lighthouse.

GETTING THERE From the A82 take the ferry from Corran to Ardgour, the A861 for 25 miles to Salen, then a left on to the B8007. On reaching Kilchoan, follow the lane along the coast, and the site is near the end of this.

PUBLIC TRANSPORT City Link buses (08705 505050) and trains (Scotrail; 01397 703791) run to Fort William, from where Shiel Buses run a daily service to Kilchoan Post Office (01967 431272), which is less than a mile from the campsite.

OPEN April–September

THE DAMAGE Adults £9; children (5–14yrs) £4; under-5s free. Dogs 50p. Electric hook-ups £4.

Cleadale Campsite

13 Cleadale, Isle of Eigg PH42 4RL   01687 482480   eiggorganics.co.uk

Nothing can prepare you for the view at Cleadale. Admittedly, the journey here does a good job of warming you up – especially if you see dolphins, minke whales or an orca on the ferry over. And the island of Eigg itself gets ever more spectacular as you approach, with its serried banks of sheer cliffs and the insolent snub nose of An Sgurr towering over the harbour. Any geologists on your boat will be in heaven; birdwatchers may well be spontaneously combusting. But it's only when the local minibus rattles its way up and over the ludicrous ribbon of tarmac that passes for a road on the island and drops you down into the cluster of crofts in the northern corner that you really get it.

First you look seawards. Ah, you think, look at that – a sweep of green land, a white sand beach, a shining Hebridean sound and the jagged crown of the cuillin of Rum. JRR Tolkien holidayed here, and you can bet he had Rum in mind when he imagined the Misty Mountain. It's amazing. Then you heft your bag and turn to look at the campsite – and realise you will be staying at the bottom of a vast and curving cliff, an amphitheatre tiered infinitely steeply as if for the sole purpose of giving the eagles a braw place from which to observe the sunset.

The campsite itself is as wild and wonderful as its setting. The pitches aren't the flattest and the dish-washing sink is outdoors. But if you're the kind of person who likes watching buzzards coast from the cliffs as you wash the pasta sauce from your plate, you'll love the view at Cleadale.

COOL FACTOR That view... (sigh).

WHO'S IN Tents – yes. Campervans, caravans, big groups, young groups, dogs – no.

ON SITE 10 pitches, no electrical hook-ups – this is as close to wild camping as a campsite gets. There are 2 composting loos (one of which would win a national 'Loo With a View' competition by a mile). There is also a yurt (sleeps 3) and a self-catering bothy from the original croft cattle shed (sleeps 4; open all year). The only shop on Eigg is on the other side of the island, so make sure you bring supplies. The site does sell free-range eggs and home-grown seasonal organic vegetables, though, plus pizzas on selected nights (see *Food & Drink*).

OFF SITE 2 excellent beaches within 15 minutes' walk. One of which, the Singing Sands, has natural arches, caves and waterfalls to explore. The crofting museum a couple of houses along is fascinating. Take the path just past the Lageorna restaurant up on to the cliffs for an airy and unforgettable circular walk. The locals love a good ceilidh, so check out if there's one happening and join in.

FOOD & DRINK On selected nights you can order pizzas, freshly cooked in the campsite's new pizza oven or, for a special treat, the restaurant Lageorna (01687 482405) is a 2-minute walk away and offers fine food with a friendly atmosphere (plus windows that make the most of the setting).

GETTING THERE A minibus service travels between the pier and Cleadale twice a day. You can hire bikes (call Jamie on 01687 482405) and residents are happy to give lifts if you stick your thumb out. There's usually plenty of traffic around the hour before and the hour after boats come in. Or you can walk to the croft from the pier (about an hour).

OPEN March–October.

THE DAMAGE Adults £6, under-16s free. Showers are available on request from the house for £2. Yurt £50 a night. Bothy £30.

Invercaimbe

Arisaig, Inverness-shire PH39 4NT   01687 450375   invercaimbecaravansite.co.uk

Invercaimbe might be the only campsite in the country that is linked to the beach by a children's slide. Well, that's just one way on to the sand that seems to surround the site. Actually you can also jump, step or flop down from your pitch straight on to the bright white strand.

This working croft has been in the same family for 270 years and, as soon as you arrive, you'll see why they've been so keen to hang on to it. The perfect little beaches curve like scallop shells around two sides of the headland and open on to a rocky foreshore. Here, as the tide goes out, you'll discover a mysterious playground of sands, lagoons and rock pools. You can't help but feel 10 years old here; the urge to dig canals and take crabs hostage is all but irresistible. Even if you only dangle your feet in the cool turquoise waters you'll instantly feel your cares washing away.

The sea is so much a part of this site that everyone becomes a little amphibious. Couples don wetsuits and splash through the rising shallows like dolphins; children taunt the incoming waves like oystercatchers; kayakers awkwardly launch themselves into the foam where they become as sleek as seals. Then, as the sun begins to drop drowsily into the west, most people grab a cup of something and perch on the rocks to watch one of the most spectacular sunsets in the land. It's hard to take your eyes off the kaleidoscope of colour but you must be careful that you don't let it capture your spirit completely. After all, where do you think mermaids come from?

COOL FACTOR White sands, shallow lagoons, knockout views over the sea to Skye and dramatic sunsets.

WHO'S IN Tents, campervans, caravans, groups, dogs – yes.

ON SITE 18 pitches, 16 hook-ups. There are 4 toilets, 2 showers, a laundry and dish-washing room. Campfires allowed. The best way to book a pitch is to text Joyce, who also keeps a freezer stocked with essentials: burgers, buns, veg, ice-cream, and beef reared on the croft – about as organic as you can get.

OFF SITE Ferries run from Arisaig and Mallaig to visit the beautiful nearby small isles and also Skye – operators are Arisaig Marine (01687 450224) or Cal Mac (0800 066 5000). Arisaig Marine also runs sealife-watching trips. There are walks along the side of Loch Morar and The Jacobite steam train runs from Mallaig (9 miles away), which is worth visiting in itself to try some fresh fish or just watch the boats come and go from the working harbour. The Ardnamurchan Lighthouse (01972 510210) is also worth a tour.

FOOD & DRINK Treat yourself to lunch or supper just 10 minutes' walk up the hill at the stunningly situated Cnoc na Faire (01687 450249), a stylish spot with cracking views. The Café Rhu (01687 450707) in Arisaig, 2 miles away, is fab for both quick bites and more leisurely meals. Whether you eat in the bar or the restaurant of The Arisaig Hotel (01687 450210) you will find a medley of fresh seafood. The creamy East Coast Cullen Skink and dish of Loch-Nan-Uamh mussels are both first class.

GETTING THERE Take the A830 from Fort William through Glenfinnan towards Mallaig. After you pass through Arisaig look out for the signposts to Invercaimbe.

PUBLIC TRANSPORT The Shiel Bus service (01967 431272) running between Fort William and Mallaig, passes Invercaimbe campsite along the A830. Ask and they can drop you off.

OPEN March–October.

THE DAMAGE A pitch and 2 people from £12 per night.

Camus More

Kilmuir, Near Uig, Isle of Skye IV51 9YS   01470 552312

The Isle of Skye has always been one of the more romantic spots of Scotland, the epitome of the tartan and heather view of the Highlands and Islands. This is partly because it's always been the most accessible island from the mainland, so it's a little more well known – and well worn – than the outer isles. Even before the stylish Skye Bridge was built and the tolls abolished, Skye was only a short ferry trip from Kyle of Lochalsh. And it was the first of the Hebrides to have Sunday sailings, in 1964; something that still causes controversy with other islands today.

Skye's reputation is for its scenery, from the ragged Cuillins to the ridges of Trotternish, and for its association with Bonnie Prince Charlie. After his defeat at the Battle of Culloden in 1746 the fleeing prince, dressed in drag, was rowed across from Benbecula by a local lass, Flora MacDonald. He gave her a locket in thanks and hoped they'd meet again. They never did. He fled to live out his days as an exile in Rome while she was arrested and sent to the Tower of London. She was later released and emigrated to North Carolina and has gone down in history as a plucky and rosy-cheeked heroine.

Camus More, in the small crafting community of Bornesketaig, has been in the MacDonald family for four generations and Iain and Bryony have lived here full time since 1989. They started up the small campsite a good 20-odd years ago, but have managed to keep it fairly under the radar (they don't own a computer so have no website), known only to a small band of aficionados and the occasional lost soul who stumbles here by mistake.

There are only a dozen or so pitches, shaved out of the long grass and separated from the beach by a low stone wall. The site is on the Ray Mears side of basic, with just two loos and an outdoor sink for washing – and it's cold water only – but then somehow it seems in keeping with the sparse surroundings. Behind the site the land sweeps slowly upwards, dotted with houses from the old to the new, up towards the cliffs of the Trotternish Ridge. This jagged range defines the north of Skye as surely as the Cuillins do the south. There's a grand road right up through the middle of the mountains that's worth trying (by bike if you're feeling fit and brave) for the fantastic views down the eastern side of Skye and out over Staffin Island.

From the site at Camus More, if you're lucky or patient – probably both – you might spot a golden eagle over the hills to the south, a family of otters round the headland or even the occasional school of basking sharks out in the bay, though more likely you'll just get stared at by all the cows in the back field.

If you're not treated to a show by the local wildlife, then you can at least expect a great sunset. The site looks straight across the Little Minch towards Harris and the Uists and, as the long summer evenings draw to a close here, the sun sinks down behind the line of the Outer Hebrides and you can almost count the islands poking from the fiery sea as they taper off to the south. It's classic Skye and this is why people can't help but be drawn back to the island – including Flora MacDonald, who came home and ended her days here, perhaps enjoying the very same sunset views.

COOL FACTOR A true taste of the remote crofting life in one of the lesser-known parts of Skye.

WHO'S IN Tents, campervans, caravans, dogs – yes.

ON SITE A dozen or so grass pitches, no electrical hook-ups. Facilities are fairly basic. There's 1 male and 1 female loo with washbasin and cold water only. There's an outside twin sink with a drinking-water tap and a shed with table and chairs, a fridge and a couple of power points for battery/mobile recharging. Campfires permitted. Boat launching permitted.

OFF SITE The Flora MacDonald memorial and the Skye Museum of Island Life (01470 552206) are over the hill and worth a visit for anyone who's ever heard of Bonnie Prince Charlie being rowed in a boat over the sea to Skye. It's around 2 miles away and best reached via a pleasant walk along the coast, which also takes in the Cave of Gold on the headland – Skye's answer to Fingal's cave on Staffa. The rock formations around it are also the same (if far smaller) as the famous Giant's Causeway in Northern Ireland. From campsite to cave is a delightful short walk and it's a great place for a picnic, although the final, pathless coastal slope down to it is very steep and dangerous, requiring great care. Best to stay on the main path to be safe if it's windy or wet.

FOOD & DRINK The Duntulm Castle Hotel (01470 552213) is fine for a pint but doesn't offer anything particularly special otherwise; you might be better off making your own fun – and food – back at the site.

GETTING THERE From Uig at the end of the A87 follow the A855 towards Kilmuir. At Kilvaxter turn left at the signpost for Bornesketaig. Follow the road down the hill and turn left at the wee crossroads (by the red postbox). The site is by the sea on the right.

PUBLIC TRANSPORT Stagecoach bus 57 (A or C) does a loop past Kilmuir from Portree. From Kilmuir it's a mile's walk to the campsite.

OPEN Mid May–mid September.

THE DAMAGE A tent with 2 adults costs £6. The price goes up depending on extra campers.

Sands

Sands Caravan and Camping, Gairloch, Wester Ross IV21 2DL   01445 712152   sandscaravanandcamping.co.uk

The shop at Sands is possibly the most remarkably stocked campsite store in the country. So much so that, as you check in, you might think the owners James and Marie have gone a wee bit over the top. But then you pitch your tent, breathe in the sea air, look out through the dune grass at the islands and mountains and realise that venison steaks, champagne and colourful kites are EXACTLY what you need right now.

That's the thing about Sands – it keeps surprising you. The winding road that leads north out of Gairloch seems to be heading nowhere, then a sliver of grassy land gradually unfolds into a wide and welcoming apron bordered by swooping dunes and an epic seascape. Driving in, your first impressions are of a large caravan site, but campers have their own area of rolling duneland with plenty of tent-sized pockets for them to hide away in. This starts just down a winding track from the shop, and it's worth continuing along to check out the whole site before choosing your spot. Pitches range from secluded hollows to breezy eyries, while the spots in the southern corner are ideally placed by the site's own slipway – perfect for launching kayaks and embarking upon other watery adventures.

There are also 12 heated wooden wigwams should you fancy taking it a little easier. These come with firepits (campfires are not allowed anywhere else on the campsite, though right down by the waterside is fine) and sublime views of the sunset as standard. Wherever you are, though, it won't be long before you're winding your way through the dunes and down on to the beach to paddle in the irresistibly turquoise water. And even if this is surprisingly cold, don't worry – the shop sells wetsuits, too.

The beach, of course, is the campsite's glory. During the day its gently sloping sands call one and all for a happy shift of castle-building, swimming and general larking about. Then, when your work is done, you can perch in the grass at the top of the dunes, taking pride in your achievements and watching the blazing sunset over the far tip of Skye. This is a dreamer's place and, as the sun finally slides into the western ocean, the island of Longa drops into shadow, becoming a humpbacked Scottish sea monster, settling down to rest for the night.

With a beach to dig up, dunes to jump down, rocks to graze knees on and woods to go heffalump-hunting in, it's ironic that the campsite also has an adventure playground – it's not like it needs one. However, it's a beauty, and is set right in the middle of the site, forming the perfect spot for young teens to gather in and eye each other sheepishly while their parents read the paper. Arrive when the sun is shining and you might also wonder why there is a games room. Well, it has been known to rain in the north-west of Scotland, and you may find yourself very glad of the owners' foresight. There is also a large indoor cooking and washing-up area, complete with several benches, and a small onsite café where you can pick up your morning cuppa. James and Marie are also planning to lay out a few mountain-bike tracks on some adjacent land. Like there isn't enough to do here already....

COOL FACTOR Family-friendly dune setting with serene views of Skye and the Hebrides.

WHO'S IN Tents, campervans, caravans, dogs (on leads) – yes.

ON SITE 2 of the 3 wash-blocks were recently refurbished and facilities are well kept. There is a large indoor kitchen and dining space, the barn café, a dish-washing area, electrical hook-ups, a laundry, a games room, plus bike and canoe hire and a children's adventure playground. The (fully licensed) shop is very well stocked. Campfires permitted on the beach only, plus in the pits outside the 12 wooden wigwams.

OFF SITE The beautiful path to Flowerdale Falls, which are located a mile south of Gairloch (3 miles from the campsite), offers an energetic family ramble. The Gairloch Heritage Museum (01445 712287) is a great local museum that will have you stepping back in time to soak up some local history. Beinn Eighe National Nature Reserve (14 miles), Scotland's oldest reserve, established in 1951, offers woodland trails and mountain walks, all situated within the expansive and beautiful ancient pine forests surrounding Loch Maree.

FOOD & DRINK The Mountain Coffee Company in Gairloch (01445 712316) has a terrific selection of outdoor and adventure books, and the cakes are pretty thrilling, too. The food at The Old Inn at Flowerdale (01445 712006) is worth seeking out, and tastes particularly delicious if you sit outside and enjoy it under the trees by the river. Pootle around the loch to The Badachro Inn (01445 741255), which snuggles by the seashore in a sheltered bay, where you can choose from 50 malt whiskies or simply enjoy a pint of the local ale by open fires and watch the boats come and go.

GETTING THERE Take the A832 to Gairloch. From there follow the B8021 coastal road north towards Melvaig. Sands is 4 miles along this road on the left.

PUBLIC TRANSPORT There is a daily bus from Inverness to Gairloch, from where you will need to walk or hitch the final 4 miles to the site.

OPEN April–September.

THE DAMAGE A pitch and 2 people £18–£20. Extra adults £8, children (5–16yrs) £2.50, under-5s free.

Badrallach

Croft 9, Badrallach, Dundonnell, Ross-shire IV23 2QP   07435 123190   badrallach.com

How does it feel to get to the end of a track that's eight miles from the nearest main road, in a remote corner of north-west Scotland? That's a question that Badrallach's owners, Owen and Christy, have put a great deal of thought and effort into answering.

To start with, if you've come this far, there's a pretty good chance you'll be aiming to get away from it all – including other people. So there are individual camping pitches hidden away between bushes and rowan thicket. A web of little paths and bridges that will have younger campers playing hide-and-seek for hours allows you to navigate between them, while firepits – the best places to sit, rest and simply gaze at the amazing scenery – are duly provided at every pitch.

Around the campsite, mountains rise into the north and east. Venture out and you may well return wet/muddy/sweaty/all three in the course of a day, so you want showers that do more than tickle and tease. The loo block itself may be in an old farm building, but it is still one of the brightest and most welcoming washing facilities we've seen. And finally, since this part of the world is the haunt of the mischievous highland midge, Badrallach Campsite boasts a hearty stock of midge repellents, nets and hats, plus it offers yet more encouragement to light that evening campfire.

Nature has also laid on a smorgasbord of adventures for you to savour. Sit at Badrallach for any length of time and you'll become fascinated by mighty An Teallach, the mountain that sits over the loch, hunching its shoulders and glowering. If you do climb this splendid hill, remember it is one of the most precipitous ridges of any mountain in Britain and you should be fully prepared (in mind as well as body). If you fancy a more casual wander, there are paths running directly from the campsite along the foreshore and up to Beinn Ghobhlach, the hill behind the site.

The campsite also looks over Little Loch Broom, which is reached by a short path. If you are a paddle-fanatic you'll find the crinkled coastline fascinating to explore in the campsite's kayak, and site warden Chris Davidson – a Highlander who's been scouring this coast his whole life – is happy to lend advice if you've laden your car with fishing tackle too. A little further along the coast is Scoraig, one of the most remote communities in Britain, which is only accessible by boat or a five-mile walk. Kayaking there takes a little while, but that's just the kind of thing you'll have time for.

Indeed a slower pace of life is just the appeal of this part of Scotland. It's certainly something that Owen loves about the place. A qualified botanist, herbalist and wilderness therapist, he has recently begun running nature-oriented workshops at the campsite, incorporating herbal medicine, stress-management and creative approaches such as music, art and writing. And, whether you come here to partake in soothing stress-relief or simply want a loch-side tent pitch, once you've been at Badrallach for a few days you, too, will settle into a new rhythm of existing. Time drifts here and pulls you along with it. So when you're finally packing up, you'll find yourself asking a very different question – how will it feel when you return to the world at the end of the road eight miles away?

COOL FACTOR Where the end of the road is also the start of your adventure.

WHO'S IN Tents, groups, dogs – yes. Caravans and campervans (maximum 3 at any one time; maximum length 6m) – yes. Caravans must be towed by four-wheel-drive vehicles.

ON SITE 20 grass pitches on a gently sloping field. 3 electrical hook-ups; 2 ladies', 2 gents' and 1 disabled loo, plus 2 unisex showers. Communal kitchen (including washing-up area and fridge) and a washing line. If not booked by a group, the bothy facilities can be used by campers: eating area, wood-burning stove, darts, board games, tourist info, small library and comfy settee. Kayaks, wooden dinghy and a Zodiac motorboat available for hire. Campfires allowed; firepits provided on half of the pitches. BBQs must be off the grass. You can also rent the gas-lit cottage for a more luxurious stay.

OFF SITE The site is a great place for walking, climbing and kayaking – there is a colony of seals living just a quick paddle away, often dozing on the rocks or popping up for a peak. Corrieshalloch Gorge is a spectacular chasm that you can reach easily by road (20 minutes). There's also An Teallach (8 miles away) – 'Scotland's finest ridge walk', the 635m Beinn Ghobhlach just behind the campsite and a beautiful 5-mile loch-side stroll to the roadless, off-grid community of Scoraig.

FOOD & DRINK It's a long way to the nearest shop, so come prepared. The Dundonnell Hotel (01854 633204; 7½ miles away) has a restaurant and a bar with frequent live music.

GETTING THERE Take the A9 north from Inverness, then the A835 to Ullapool; 10 miles from Ullapool at Braemore Junction turn left on to the A832. Follow this for 10 miles then turn right on to the single-track Badrallach road for approximately 7 miles.

OPEN All year.

THE DAMAGE Adults £5, children (2–16yrs) £2.50, under-2s free. Vehicles £2.50; camper or caravan £2.50; electricity £3.

Lickisto Blackhouse

1 Lickisto, Isle of Harris HS3 3EL   01859 530485

Ever been to a party where you meet someone and you keep thinking you ought to be talking to your old pals but you're having so much fun that you spend the whole night happily wittering to your new chum? Lickisto is the campsite equivalent of that magnetic personality.

On the eastern coast of Harris, perched snugly above a sea loch, this campsite is perfect for exploring the island, from the wilds of the east coast or the breathtaking beaches of the west, but many campers barely leave the site, so drawn are they to its rock-star charisma.

Harvey and John, Lickisto's resourceful owners, have transformed a rough and rocky croft into a relaxing retreat, where the love they have lavished on their labours can be clearly seen and felt. Harvey is a fancy cook and bakes fresh bread for the camping guests every day before going off to work at his hair salon in Tarbert, while John does all the handywork. Since acquiring Lickisto Blackhouse a decade or so ago, they've been slowly converting the place into one of the finest little campsites in the country.

For those looking for a private place to pop the tent there is plenty of choice. The camping pitches are personally cut by John and are separated from each other by wild grasses and heather, giving everyone their own individual space; plus there are a couple of yurts for lazybones, pitched high up on the site to give splendid ocean views. Each comes with a wood-burning stove, running water, futons (with linen), gas stove, carpets and candles. Harvey even pops a homemade loaf in, so don't forget your butter and jam.

The site has its own restored blackhouse where you can cook a meal, play Jenga, have a shower or simply slouch on a leather sofa and dream. Pluck a fishing rod from the wall and you can try catching your supper from the loch. And guests are also free to enjoy the fruits (and veg) of the polytunnel – the lemon basil will be perfect should you hook a fish. Down by the sea loch there's a small landing cove if you want to turn up by boat or fancy having a waterside campfire. Around the communal table you're as likely to be rubbing shoulders with cyclists, canoeists and walkers as with people who've come by car. Lickisto is proud to be low-impact and small scale, with a roof thatched with local heather, and wooden bridges and walkways made from telegraph poles discarded at the roadside.

When you arrive, one of the owners is usually on hand to give you a tour. It's a seductive introduction and, as you wind down little paths between stands of high rushes and turn unexpected corners that reveal perfect pitches hidden behind flowering bushes, you may be forgiven for thinking your guide is actually a white rabbit in disguise, leading you into Wonderland. The resident wildfowl are only too happy to make your acquaintance and the ducks, in particular, have an engaging habit of wandering up and eyeing you in a way that clearly says, 'Have you finished with that biscuit?'. Down by the water of an evening, there's a good chance you'll see a local otter making his daily commute down the loch with his supper in his mouth. Rush hour at Lickisto then – a site not to be missed.

COOL FACTOR A stunning oasis in the spectacular lunar landscape of Harris.

WHO'S IN Tents, campervans, dogs – yes. Caravans, big groups – no.

ON SITE 15 pitches, 4 campervan pitches with hook-ups and 2 yurts. 'Bathroom byres' with 3 loos, 3 showers and loads of character. Blackhouse where campers can cook, chat and chill. The site is better suited to small or medium-sized tents: large 'multipods' could find it difficult to pitch. A polytunnel with home-grown veg and herbs is open for campers. Bring midge repellent. Campfires are allowed on the foreshore.

OFF SITE There are several art galleries on the east coast of Harris. You'll see why when you drive along the road. Pick up some genuine Harris Tweed in the shop at Tarbert. Visit the eagle observatory on the road to Huisinish and make the effort to visit the Standing Stones at Callanish – they are older than Stonehenge and have an impressive visitor centre with an exhibition and café (01851 621422). The downside is that it's 40 miles or so north of Lickisto on the Isle of Lewis, so it's a day trip, but a worthwhile one (see p.216).

FOOD & DRINK Soak up some inspiration (and stunning home-baking) at the nearby Skoon Art Café (01859 530268). The Temple Café in Northton (07876 340416) is also worth a stop, making delicious food in as tiny a kitchen as you'll ever see. Back in Tarbert, the bar at The Hotel Hebrides (01859 502364) used to be a dive but has been done up to look like a Battersea wine bar.

GETTING THERE From Tarbert take the A859 south, heading for Leverburgh. After about 4½ miles turn left at the sign for Roghadal. Follow the single-track road for 2½ miles, cross the bridge and, as you climb the hill, just before the bus stop, turn left. There are small discreet camping signs to help direct you.

PUBLIC TRANSPORT The W13 bus runs from Tarbert Pier to Leverburgh, stopping not far from the campsite if you ask.

OPEN March–October (but, by arrangement, you can stay any time of the year).

THE DAMAGE Adults £12, children £6, littl'uns free. Yurt and 2 people £70 (extra person £20, larger kids £10).

Cnip Grazing

Cnip, Uig, Isle of Lewis HS2 9HS   01851 672332

If you've never felt like you've reached the end of the earth then come to Traigh na Beirigh (don't try to pronounce it) near Cnip (pronounced 'neep'). This tiny crofting community on the western coast of Lewis in the Outer Hebrides seems like the last place on earth. In reality, if you'd kept on going west you'd eventually end up on the Labrador Coast of Newfoundland (where there's probably someone looking east feeling the same as you) but you'd never guess it standing on the dunes of Traigh na Beirigh gazing out over the aqua-blue water. It feels like the end of everywhere you've ever been. And that, of course, is the attraction. Even the cluster of cottages that comprise Cnip is over the hill in the neighbouring bay, so the only thing to disturb the peace is that occasional bang of a grousing gun in the hills behind and the sound of the waves on the beach.

Traigh na Beirigh is the name of the bay on whose grassy dunes the campsite sits and the site is owned by the Cnip villagers through a community trust. The village itself is 40 miles from Lewis's only real town, Stornoway, over miles of captivating emptiness in which rocks poke up through the threadbare soil like elbows through an old tweed jacket. Even in the summer, the weather on Lewis can be cold and harsh and the landscape elemental and bleak. And so the bay, when it comes, is something of a surprise. The road from Cnip climbs the shoulder of the hill and, as you crest the brow, the brilliant blue of the bay is suddenly there before you with its scimitar of white sand fringed with grass.

Compared with some of Scotland's other bays, though, Traigh na Beirigh is modest. If you really want to stretch your legs, then head for Uig Sands, four miles south of Cnip. It's an extravagant cove where the low tide retreats for miles out to sea and leaves a rippled tract of golden sand. It was here that a cow accidentally found the Lewis Chessmen in 1831. Made by the Vikings from walrus ivory, these 12th-century chess pieces were discovered among the sands and are now in the National Museum in Edinburgh.

Old though the ancient chessmen are, even they are new kids on the block in comparison with Lewis' main attraction, the Standing Stones at Calanais (Callanish). These swirling spires of Lewisian gneiss, the oldest rock in Britain, have the gnarled look of petrified oak trunks. Set in the shape of a Celtic cross, they are older than Stonehenge and just as baffling. The runic allure of them attracts its fair share of hiking hippies, who come to commune with the stones, much to the frustration of photographers in search of that cherished shot (and much to the amusement of the incurious sheep). Neither can ruin the simple grandeur of Calanais, though, particularly as dusk begins to fall. If you can get a shot of the stones at sunset, it will definitely be one to keep.

Back at Cnip, sunrise over the waters of the bay is another finger-clicking moment to cherish long after you've gone home to tell your friends all about your stay at the end of the earth.

COOL FACTOR Stunning setting at the very end of the world.

WHO'S IN Tents, campervans, caravans, dogs – yes.

ON SITE Around 30 pitches; no electrical hook-ups. 1 small but serviceable toilet block with male and female facilities (1 cubicle and 2 £1-coin-operated showers each) and a dish-washing station. Recycling facility behind the toilet block. BBQ areas set among the dunes west of the campsite, along with a small football field.

OFF SITE Drive the ½-hour to ancient Callanish Standing Stones and throw in the 20-minute (each way) diversion out to Traigh Bhostadh (Bosta Beach). This white shell sand beach at the far end of the tiny Island of Great Bernera is the very spot you are looking across at from the campsite. Behind the beach lie the grazings and remains of the township of Bostaidh, which was cleared 2 centuries ago. However, humans were using this fertile land for a long time before that. The Iron-Age village excavated here has been complimented by a replica Iron-Age house built to explain the findings revealed by the local history society. During the summer the Iron-Age house is open to the public. Mounted on the far skerry is the Time and Tide Bell, one of several placed around the British coastline. The unique design creates a range of tones when the rising tide causes it to ring.

FOOD & DRINK There are more churches than there are pubs on Lewis. The Uig Community Shop, 4 miles south of Cnip at Timsgarry, is licensed and sells a decent range of beers, wines and spirits. Otherwise, best to stock up on food in advance.

GETTING THERE From Stornoway, follow the A859 to Leurbost and turn right to Achmor. Then take the B1011 to Miabhig. Take a right and follow the road through Cliobh to Cnip. Stop at house number 15 at the foot of the hill to pay.

PUBLIC TRANSPORT There is a bus service (W4) from Stornoway to Uig with a separate service for the loop road through Cnip.

OPEN April–October

THE DAMAGE £6–£15 per unit depending on size.

Scourie

Harbour Road, Scourie, Sutherland IV27 4TG   01971 502060   scouriecampsitesutherland.com

Robert Burns, Scotland's great mythologiser of the mundane and the simple, wrote odes to such humdrum things as mice, lice and haggis. But he never eulogised the Scottish midge, and with good reason. Midges are neither soft and furry nor very appetising. Besides, 'wee sleekit cow'rin'tim'rous chironomidae' doesn't scan very well.

Whereas many of Scotland's coastal campsites are too windy for midges, the sheltered bay at Scourie does, unfortunately, provide ideal flying conditions for the little blighters. However, that is no reason not to come and enjoy one of Sutherland's most tranquil sites. This region is one of the most sparsely populated in Europe and the scattered dwellings of the area's few human habitations seem to cling to the coast for safety.

Scourie is a tiny hamlet clustered around an inlet on the extreme north-west coast, 40 miles from Ullapool. The landscape here may be stark and sparse but the campsite is a little oasis of green. At first glance, you'd be forgiven for mistaking the green terraces for a nine-hole pitch-and-putt course, so immaculate is the grass. Caravans and motorhomes are confined to the areas around the amenities block, so tents have the run of the terraced pitches that extend down to the shore.

Scourie is an ideal stopping-off point between Ullapool and the far north coast around Durness, 25 miles from Scourie. From Durness, a coastal village that seems like something blown north from Cornwall by doomsday winds, a tiny boat takes you across the Kyle of Durness to rendezvous with a minibus that plies the only stretch of road in Britain not connected to any other road.

It runs the 11 miles through an area called the Parph out to Cape Wrath, the most north-easterly point of the mainland and the site of a Stevenson lighthouse (worth a nose around). It's a favourite haunt of kite-surfers, clinging to their kites as the winds try to whisk them off to Spitzbergen.

For the intrepid there is a chillingly remote coastal walk from the crumbly chocolate cliffs of Cape Wrath back to the road from Kinlochbervie. The walk takes in the fantastic beach at Sandwood Bay and is so remote that it would make even Ray Mears crave extra company. The landscape here is not so much mountainous as pockmarked with massive towers of stone rising out of moorland.

Heading south from Scourie towards Ullapool is the impressive Loch Assynt with the forlorn ruin of Ardvreck Castle sitting exposed to the whipping winds. In 1650, the Marquis of Montrose, who had continued to fight for Charles I, even after the king's execution in 1649, was led from here, trussed and bound to a horse, to Edinburgh for execution. He was placed on his horse backwards and would have had a magnificent view of the receding castle as he was led away. Forty years later, the castle was ruined after a siege and was left as it stands today, an empty but imposing shell.

After the sparseness of Sutherland, Ullapool feels like a metropolis. It's a small but bustling town and the main ferry route to the Outer Hebrides. Fresh fish is landed by a small fleet of brightly coloured trawlers, so it's no surprise that Ullapool boasts one of the best chippies in Britain – known only as The Chippy. A name whose simplicity Robert Burns would no doubt have admired.

COOL FACTOR Peace and tranquillity on impeccably flat, green pitches amid the far north-west coast's rugged beauty.

WHO'S IN Tents, campervans, caravans, dogs – yes.

ON SITE Well-drained pitches, hardstanding options and electrical hook-ups. Ablutions block with toilets, showers and basins. Dish-washing and laundry also available. Chemical disposal point. Onsite café/bar.

OFF SITE Measuring about 1 x 1½ miles, Handa Island is a Site of Special Scientific Interest and is looked after as a nature reserve by the Scottish Wildlife Trust. Up until the mid 19th century, Handa supported a relatively large population for its size – in the census of 1841, 63 people lived there. The islanders worked the crofts and fished, while abundant bird life provided an additional resource – eggs were eaten, houses were lit by burning fulmar oil and bird feathers were traded for supplies. The potato famine of 1848 eventually led all the residents to emigrate, but the birds, of course, stayed on. Today there is some 150 species on the island, including over 100,000 resident guillemots. Take a boat out from Tarbert Pier (07780 967800) and watch the puffins, fulmers and shags, among others.

FOOD & DRINK The Anchorage pub onsite has a good atmosphere and serves up cracking food, while The Scourie Hotel (01971 502396), 2 minutes' walk away, serves real ale (with a changing selection of guest ales) and decent pub grub but in a rather fatigued setting. There's a small supermarket in Scourie.

GETTING THERE From Ullapool follow the A834 north to Ledmore Junction and turn left on to the A837. Along the shores of Loch Assynt, turn right up the hill on to the A894 and it's another 17 miles before you hit Scourie.

PUBLIC TRANSPORT Buses N67 and S67 run north from Inverness via Ullapool and up the A838 to Scourie.

OPEN March–September.

THE DAMAGE Adults £8, first 2 children (6–16yrs) £4, all others and all under-6s free. Electricity £4.

Sango Sands

Durness, Sutherland IV27 4PP   01971 511726   sangosands.com

Sutherland is the least populated place in Britain; and while journeying north to reach the isolated community of Durness, cityslickers on a rare trip north may find the emptiness and desolation slightly unnerving. For this reason, when the wide-eyed traveller finally rides into the wee village of Durness (population 400) it can feel like somewhere much, much bigger.

Travelling through the beautiful, slightly brutal scenery of this top north-western corner of Scotland is a sensational experience and, taken slowly (stopping off at the other *Cool Camping* sites along the west coast, perhaps), it's a journey that will surprise, delight and sometimes shock. Once any sober mind has made it past Ullapool, it will be hard-pressed to recall any other place in Britain that quite captures the same essence of wilderness.

This is the setting for Sango Sands. It wouldn't matter if this campsite doubled up as the local bus shelter, for it offers succour to the weary traveller when it seems that the world has ended which, in effect, it does just here.

Sango Sands teeters on the northern edge of Britain in glorious fashion, a fitting end to the trek through all that emptiness – a view out to infinity. Its unique north-facing location at the very top of Scotland means that in summer you can watch the sun both rise and set over the ocean. That is if you aren't lying in your sleeping bag, exhausted from all the outdoor adventuring that you can't help yourself doing in this wild and windswept corner of the land.

If you can drag your eyes away from the view of mountains on two-and-a-half sides, and the endless ocean on the other three (really, this is fact, not an optical illusion) then the campsite itself is fairly ordinary. But you can't and it isn't.

There are several fields to camp in and the most picturesque spots are by the steep slopes above the beaches. There are other thoughtfully prepared areas for tents too, which give children ample room to kick a ball around away from nearby cars. And though there are caravans littering the site in places, they're almost invisible because the scenery is so magnificently big. The toilet blocks, of which there are several, are fine, though lengthy details of hot showers and clean basins slightly miss the point of why this campsite is so superb; as television fans would say, it's all about location, location, location.

The place boasts an embarrassment of sandy blessings with not one but two spectacular beaches easily reached by tracks from the site. The land and sea might meet here, but it's clear that they don't really get on. The beach is scattered with black rocks carved from ancient cliffs by centuries of northern storms. The power of the waves makes it a favourite spot of surfers, and you can hire boards nearby if you fancy joining in. Or, if the waves aren't too pounding, it is possible to swim.

That's the thing about Durness: it may be remote, but there's a lot to do. A few miles west is the aptly named Cape Wrath, which you can visit by catching a ferry and then a minibus – there's a lighthouse, the highest sea cliffs in Britain and a thrilling sense of freedom. Then you can return to your tent on its clifftop eyrie and stay awake for that late, late sunset.

COOL FACTOR Amazing scenery and location, teetering on one of Britain's northernmost tips.

WHO'S IN Tents, campervans, caravans, groups, dogs – yes.

ON SITE 120+ pitches, 64 electrical hook-ups. 3 wash-blocks, 1 solely dedicated to showers. Waste disposal, dishwashing and laundry facilities. Communal kitchen for all campers to use with free gas. Campers need to book in advance if a hook-up is required. No campfires. Note: although the campsite itself is dog-friendly, The Oasis Bar on the campsite is not.

OFF SITE The beach surrounding the site is great for surfing. Balnakiel craft village is an old MOD station that now has lots of individual galleries, cafés and workshops. Durness golf course welcomes visitors and has a terrific last hole over the ocean. Smoo Cave is the largest sea cave in Britain and is just a 15-minute walk away. There is a peaceful public garden dedicated to John Lennon in Durness village – he regularly holidayed here as a boy. Cape Wrath (the most north-westerly point in mainland Britain, 15 miles away) is also an option, involving a ferry and minibus ride. Visit the lighthouse and walk the wild and wonderful coastal trail – the starting point for the 200-mile-long Cape Wrath Trail to Fort William.

FOOD & DRINK The Oasis Bar and restaurant, managed by the campsite owners, offers great food and local music, plus it's right next to the site. For what is audaciously billed as 'the best hot chocolate in the world', head to Cocoa Mountain Balnakeil (01971 511233). This spectacularly set café and chocolaterie specialises in the brown stuff, from artisan truffles to its famous 'Mountain Mocha'.

GETTING THERE This is the far north-western edge of Scotland – every route here is beautiful, but the quickest is probably the A9 north beyond Inverness then the A836 and A838 to Durness.

PUBLIC TRANSPORT There's a regular but infrequent bus service from Inverness. See travelinescotland.com for times.

OPEN April–October. Camping available at other times but without facilities.

THE DAMAGE Adults £9, plus first child (5–15yrs) £6, second child £4, additional children (and under-5s) free. Electricity £4.

Dunnet Bay

Dunnet, Thurso, Caithness KW14 8XD 01847 821319 caravanclub.co.uk

When you take it at face-value, this site should be everything that *Cool Camping* is not: a council-owned site, run by the Caravan Club, with wardens in mint-green uniforms, and rules everywhere.

Now it's true that, at the height of summer, it can seem like Caravan City, with room for only a few tents jammed up against the dunes. But therein lies the secret. The site is slap-bang next to the sand dunes of a huge sweeping bay. Long stalks of dune grass practically reach over a small wooden fence to touch your tent.

The restless waves of the Pentland Firth attract surfers from far and wide. But Dunnet Bay is one of the north coast's trump cards. With a mile or more of white sand stretching like a crescent moon to the cliffs of Dunnet Head, the most northerly point of mainland Britain, it's a spectacular setting. With a bit of sunshine, a few tinnies of beer and the odd shout of 'Ripper, mate!' you could swear you were on Bondi Beach in Australia. Well, almost.

For those with a head for heights, there's a road roaming for five miles over bleak and brown scrubland up towards the clifftop at Dunnet Head. Up there is the lighthouse built by Robert Louis Stevenson's grandfather, with views over Gills Bay and across the channel between the headland and Scapa Flow in the Orkneys. On a clear day, you can see the breadth of Scotland from up here – from Cape Wrath in the east to John o'Groats in the west – and it's worth putting up with a few too many caravans at the campsite for that alone.

COOL FACTOR Beautiful sandy bay and grassy dunes among which to pitch your tent.

WHO'S IN Tents, campervans, caravans, dogs (on a lead at all times), non-members – yes.

ON SITE 56 pitches (a mix of grass and hardstandings) with electrical hook-ups available. Pristinely kept toilets and hot showers. Dish-washing and laundry facilities. Wheelchair access and disabled shower room. Motorhome service point. Wi-Fi near the reception area. No campfires, but BBQs are permitted provided they are raised off the grass.

OFF SITE A day-trip over to Orkney from John o'Groats or Scrabster won't disappoint – you can hop the whole string of islands by boat and coach. If you're a keen birdwatcher, take a ferry trip around the Stacks of Duncansby for the chance to see kittiwakes, fulmars, guillemots, razorbills, puffins and, of course, plenty of sea gulls. If it rains, visit Mary-Ann's cottage in Dunnet village. It's an old croft, left intact after the death of its 93-year-old owner – and she had kept it just as her grandfather had.

FOOD & DRINK The lounge bar at The Northern Sands Hotel (01651 842214), half a mile away, has leather chairs and wood panelling and serves a decent pint and excellent sandwiches. For those who want a little more rock with their roll, head over to Thurso for Top Joe's at The Central Hotel (01847 893129).

GETTING THERE Follow the A836 for 7 miles from Thurso to Dunnet Bay. The site is between the road and the dunes.

PUBLIC TRANSPORT A regular daily bus service runs from Thurso to Dunnet (except on Sundays).

OPEN April–October.

THE DAMAGE Pitch and 2 people from £21.20 per night.

Glamping Alternatives

Cotna Eco Retreat

Gorran, Cornwall   01726 844867   cotna.co.uk

Streams running through this 10-acre smallholding – home to hens, horses and vegetable-filled poly-tunnels – trickle towards the quaint harbour village of Mevagissey, two miles away. The beaches of Gorran Haven, Hemmick and Vault are closer still and an easy half hour walk from your yurt. Furnished with a double bed, wood-burner and cooking facilities, the two Mongolian-style structures are also joined by a cosy shepherd's hut and an atmospheric straw-bale studio, with rough, honey-coloured interior walls housing a kitchen, brass-bedded bedroom and an en-suite bathroom. The local pub, meanwhile, built in 1837 and run by the original proprietor's great-great-grandson, is a five-minute stroll up the track.

Free Range Escapes

St Kew, Cornwall   freerangeescapes.co.uk

Bulging blackberry bushes, ivy-clad oaks and an emerald, spring-fed lagoon have returned this former quarry to a natural wonderland. Set in a flat clearing – once part of the quarry's old railway line – a single, classically designed shepherd's hut features an in-built double bed, exposed ash beams and a Windy Smith wood-burner, while tiny details – from old-style brass light fittings to binoculars and bird books – add a thoroughly homely feel. Some of the vast 20-acre space is shared with guests of an adjoining campsite but the feeling is one of wild seclusion. It's a half-hour walk to the South West Coast Path, then the same again to picturesque Port Isaac harbour.

Coastal Cabins

Hartland, Devon   01237 441407   coastal-cabins.com

Ferns, daffodils and yellow flag irises hem the pond at this two-acre glamping site on Devon's Hartland Peninsula and the place feels simultaneously manicured yet wild. It's home to 10 octagonal wooden cabins – a chic new take on the traditional beach hut – with interiors divided into three areas: a sleeping and living space, an en-suite shower room and a sleek modern kitchen. It's just over a mile to the clifftop trails that earn the site its moniker, with the nearest accessible beach a touch further. The inland village of Hartland, meanwhile, boasts several independent potteries and galleries – the beach scenes in the White Hare Gallery are a particular highlight.

Owl Valley

Bideford, Devon   01237 239204   owl-valley.co.uk

In the bottom of a North Devon valley, this off-grid wooded hideaway offers 'wild camping in style', with three bell tents and an enchanting log cabin, each set in a quiet clearing. While all have double beds, wooden cabinets, cooking wares, barbecues and their own private shower rooms, they're also delightfully free of mod-cons. Internet evenings are traded in for nights around the campfire and den-building beside the steam, while a stove-warmed recreation room has books, board games and a dartboard for rainy days. It's a mile to busy Bideford, though the famous surf beaches of Westward Ho!, Braunton Burrows, Croyde, Woolacombe and Bude are the main waterside attractions.

Knaveswell Farm

Isle of Purbeck, Dorset 01929 422918
knaveswellfarm.co.uk

Set in the landscape that once inspired Enid
Blyton, and within walking distance of the beaches
at Studland, Swanage and Durlston Bay, this 156-
acre dairy farm is one of the south-west's most
popular family glampsites. Four luxurious safari
tents are scattered across the car-free field, each
with a kitchen, two bedrooms and a living space,
plus a plush private shower room on the back
porch. Little ones can follow owners Jo and Paul
to meet the animals – yes, you can bottle-feed
lambs in spring – and there's a pair of Shetland
ponies to pet. Head to hilltop Corfe Castle for a
Famous Five-style picnic, then ride the local steam
train to Swanage Bay.

Vintage Vacations

Ryde, Isle of Wight 07802 758113 vintagevacations.co.uk

Brainchild of photographer Frazer Cunningham
and stylist Helen Carey, this supremely retro Isle of
Wight glampsite has been around for more than a
decade. That's relatively young, however, compared
to the accommodation – authentic American
Airstream trailers and classic caravans dating
back to 1946. Outside, the indelible shine of the
Airstreams reflects the lush grass of the meadow
setting while, within, not only have interiors been
impeccably restored but there are also tiny period
details – cassette players, an old whistling kettle and
retro games like Tiddlywinks and Fuzzy Felt. Ryde
and Fishbourne (both linking to Portsmouth) are
less than two miles away, while Nettlestone (three
miles), St Helens (four) and Bembridge (five) all
have good beaches.

Elmley Nature Reserve

Isle of Sheppy, Kent 07786 333331 elmleynaturereserve.co.uk

The Thames, the Medway, the English Channel and
the North Sea all converge around the 10-mile-long
Isle of Sheppy, separated from Kent by a tidal channel
and vast expanses of marshland. Despite being an SSSI
and a Ramsar site (wetlands of world importance),
Elmley National Nature Reserve is still privately run
by the central family farm. Loosely located around its
buildings, including a Victorian pitch-pine barn that's
now a cooking and social space, three handcrafted
shepherds' huts are available for stays, along with a trio
of compact wooden cabins. The latter have full-length
glass walls at one end for gazing out at wading birds
and morning mists, while all have private bathrooms
and the option of additional massage treatments.

The Shepherd's Hide

Brightlingsea, Essex 01206 302964 theshepherdshide.co.uk

Part shepherd's hut, part bird-hide and part luxury
cottage, this couples' retreat isn't exactly perched
beside the beach – the nearest is some three miles
away – yet at peak times tidal waters stretch their
fingers right into the neighbouring marshland.
Overlooking a reed-fringed channel, the hut is
furnished to impeccable detail – think biodegradable
British-made toiletries, foodie welcome hampers,
binoculars and wildlife books – with a king-sized
bed, wood-burner and plush en-suite bathroom.
Farm footpaths weave guests past a historic tidal mill
that was built in 1831 (and occasionally opens to
the public on summer weekends) while, just beyond,
Arlesford Creek offers excellent birdwatching. It takes
around 10 minutes to drive to the beaches at Clacton
on Sea and Walton on the Naze.

The Grove

Cromer, Norfolk   01263 512412   thegrovecromer.co.uk

Set on the carefully hewn lawns of The Grove, an 18th-century country house hotel, five furnished yurts offer the utmost luxury, including the likes of private, adjoining kitchens (with pizza ovens), king-sized beds and access to the hotel swimming pool. The Grove's own poly-tunnels and fruit trees help supply the inimitable restaurant – the original Georgian dining room makes for atmospheric mealtimes – and picnic hampers can be provided for days spent on the beach. Follow a private pathway at the end of the garden, through the trees and down to Cromer's Blue Flag sands, with lifeguards from May until September. It's a few hundred metres further to the town's famous pier and waterfront fish 'n' chippies.

Little Otchan Hut

Halsham, East Yorkshire   07803125687   littleotchan.co.uk

Family-run Hall Farm branched out into beer-brewing a decade ago and has now diversified into the world of glamping too. Named after the farm's most popular pint, the single, fully en-suite shepherd's hut is half a mile from the brewery itself, tucked against a flank of trees and overlooking a lily-speckled pond. Sleeping three in a double bed with a top bunk, the hut's small interior touches include a vintage-style radio, a retro microwave and a wood-burning stove. To the east is one of the longest and straightest beaches in the UK, reaching all the way north to Bridlington and curling around the Humber to form famous Spurn Point (home to a popular nature reserve) in the south. 15 miles west, meanwhile, Hull provides more urban attractions.

Amber's Bell Tents

Holt, Norfolk   07580 072861   ambersbelltents.co.uk

Amber Wykes first began her glamping enterprise – bunting-clad bell tents with double beds, wood-burners, cool-boxes and cooking equipment – in the moated garden of Norfolk's medieval Mannington Hall. Sticking to the theme of great stately homes, guests can now also stay in the grounds of 17th-century Wiveton Hall, too, located 12 miles further north and slap bang on the North Norfolk Coast. There's a pick-your-own fruit farm there (with a great little café) and it's just 200 yards to the Norfolk Coast Path, which leads to Blakeney National Nature Reserve. Continue along the waterfront trail a little further to Morston Quay to catch a seal-watching tour around Blakeney Point (see p.98).

Woodman's Huts

Haverthwaite, Cumbria   07809 402484

It's a bit of a stretch to call Woodman's Huts 'coastal', especially since the great inland attractions of the South Lakes – Windermere, Coniston Water, Grizedale Forest – are often the main appeal of the location. Yet just over a mile south the River Leven begins to widen its estuaried mouth into famous Morecambe Bay, bridged by the seaside railway line that takes passengers to Ullverston. Tucked in a small garden on the edge of the national park, the site's two over-sized shepherd's huts offer year-round glamping accommodation while a Scandi-style octagonal cabin allows guests to congregate around an open fire, complete with sheep's wool throws and hand-carved hot-chocolate mugs.

Mountain Lodge

Abergele, Conwy   01745 832242
shepherds-hut-holidays.co.uk

Atop the wooded hill behind unassuming Abergele market town and just above pleasingly plant-covered Gwrych Castle, this North Wales retreat is worthy of its name. As well as the 19th-century Gothic folly, the site boasts panoramic views of Snowdonia's Carneddau mountain range. In one location, a pair of shepherd's huts are twinned together to sleep up to five people, positioned next to a converted stable and barn space with a kitchen, shower room and social space. In another spot, a newly renovated stone cabin offers further Snowdonian solitude. If you're not hiking in the hills, bring bikes to tour the coastal cycle path, taking in nearby Llandudno and the cliffs of the Great Orme.

Bach Wen Farm

Clynnog-fawr, Gwynedd   01286 660336   bachwen.co.uk

Sitting atop the low clay cliffs that back rocky Clynnog Fawr Beach, this simple glamping set up comprises two wooden, arch-shaped pods bookending a hidden glade. Inside, each features a double bed, a mini fridge, a two-ring stove and a toasty wood-burner, but you need to bring your own bedding and cooking utensils. Campfires are permitted in the clearing beyond your pod, where you can enjoy the exceptionally starry skies that this stretch of North Wales affords. By day, meanwhile, take in the panoramic views round to the Llyn Peninsula's distant fishing villages in the south-west and Anglesey to the north. Dogs are permitted at the glampsite and the beach below is almost always quiet enough for them – and you – to run free.

Llwyndu Farm Hut

LLanaber, Gwynedd   01341 280144   thefarmhut.co.uk

Two miles from the seaside resort of Barmouth, Llwyndu Farm's traditionally shaped shepherd's hut was handcrafted by owner Stephen and features en-suite facilities, a fitted bed and a fully equipped kitchen. On the final slope of Snowdonia's Rhinog mountain range before it submerges into the Irish Sea, the hut offers breathtaking views, albeit slightly blighted by a static caravan park in the foreground. It's just a few hundred metres down to five-mile-long Morfa Dyffryn Beach, well known as Wales' official naturist beach. If you're keen to strip off, then turn right when you hit sand and walk the 30-odd minutes to the signed area. If not, keep to the beach's southern end to avoid any surprises.

Stackpole Under the Stars

Stackpole, Pembrokeshire   01646 683167
stackpoleunderthestars.wales

Within the Pembrokeshire Coast National Park but set back from the seaside proper, this inland collection of yurts, bell tents and a pod occupies the grounds of a former country manor, now reclaimed by nature and managed by the National Trust. The pod is the most luxurious option – bright, modern, fully en-suite, with mod-cons like underfloor heating and a digital television – while the wood-burner-warmed yurts have a more country home feel. There are five camping pitches too but, with an oh-so-far two-mile (45-minute) walk to the nearest beach, they didn't make the official cut for this guidebook. Award-winning Barafundle Bay is only half a mile further.

Frankshore Cabins

Tenby, Pembrokeshire 07814 035005 becksbay.co.uk

Beside the Pembrokeshire Coast Path, with Lydstep Beach a 15-minute walk west and Penally 20 minutes east, Bubbleton Farm began welcoming shepherd's hut guests in 2017. Such was the popularity that, by 2018, an old hop-picker's shack was also tastefully converted, with two separate bedrooms, en-suite facilities and a spacious, open-plan living area with lounge, dining and kitchen spaces. The nearby farm shop is an ideal pantry for barbecue meat – campfire cooking is very much allowed – while the harbour town of Tenby (two miles away) offers the freshest fish and chips, ice-cream and everything else you could need.

Runach Arainn

Lagg, Isle of Arran 01770 870515 runacharainn.com

On the southern tip of 19-mile-long Arran, the island's very first glampsite boasts three larch-framed yurts, featuring double beds and futon-style singles, plus wood-burning stoves, cooking and dining utensils and a bounty of extra blankets in case the weather gets wild. Opposite Kilmory Parish Church and within the grounds of its 17th-century former rectory, the yurts feel private but are still within walking distance of the essentials – the pub and the beach. It's a 15-minute stroll to sandy Torrylinn Beach, which looks out at distinctively conical Ailsa Craig island in the distance. Bring or rent bikes to make the most of Runach Arainn's location on the island's circular trail.

Harvest Moon

Dunbar, East Lothian 07817 968985
harvestmoonholidays.com

Less than an hour from Edinburgh, Harvest Moon Holidays has a surprisingly remote feel, accentuated by the final bumpy drive through the fields. Beyond rows of towering pines, in the dunes of Tyninghame Beach, this long-established glampsite boasts 14 different encampments – half tree houses and half safari tents. Each structure has at least two double beds, bunk beds and a double sofa bed, plus en-suite facilities and that essential wood-burning stove. Behind the dunes there's a good farm shop and a 'Kids Corner' with ponies, sheep, ducks and chickens while, in front, unfolds the endless blue-grey of the North Sea.

Sheiling Holidays

Craignure, Isle of Mull 01680 812496 shielingholidays.co.uk

Long before the word 'glamping' entered our lexicon, Isle of Mull-based Sheiling Holidays was offering nights under canvas for those not keen on pitching their own tents. Their 16 starched white shielings – like army shelters without the camouflage – may not be quite as glamorous as some places these days, but they're supremely spacious and most are en-suite. Sleeping six, they boast cookers, wood-burners, worktops, electric lighting and gas heaters, plus a breathtaking waterfront setting overlooking the Sound of Mull. You can launch your own boats and canoes, hire bikes, or simply sit and look out for wildlife – otters are resident on the rocky foreshore and porpoises regularly make an appearance.

Index

A

Aberafon, Caernafon, Gwynedd **132–133**
Amber's Bell Tents, Holt, Norfolk **233**
Ardnamurchan Campsite, Ardnamuchan Peninsula **194–197**
Argyll
  Muasdale, Tarbert, Argyll **188–191**
  Port Bàn, Tarbert, Argyll **192–193**
Arran, Isle of
  Lochranza **184–187**
  Runach Arainn, Lagg **237**

B

Bach Wen Farm, Clynnog-fawr, Gwynedd **234**
Badrallach, Dundonnell, Ross-shire **210–211**
beach games **65**
  Beachcombers' Hunt **66**
  Limbo **67**
  Sandcastle Competition **66**
  Sharks & Minnows **66**
  Shells & Stones **67**
  Water Relay Race **67**
Beacon Cottage Farm, St Agnes, Cornwall **34–37**
Beryl's Campsite, Kingsbridge, Devon **60–63**
Brittany
  Bot-Conan Lodge, Brittany **181**
  Camping du Letty, Brittany **180**
Bryher Campsite, Bryher, Isles of Scilly **20–23**

C

Cae Du Farm, Tywyn, Gwynedd **144–147**
Caffynes Farm, Lynton, Devon **56–57**
Caithness
  Dunnet Bay, Thurso, Caithness **226–227**
campervan hire **127**
  Big Tree Campervans **128**
  Bunk Campers **129**
  CamperVantastic **128**
  Indie Campers **128**
  LandCruise Motorhome Hire **129**
  Van Kampers **129**

Camping Bel Sito, Normandy **180**
Camping de l'Océan, Gironde **180**
Camping du Letty, Brittany **180**
Camping Les Chênes Verts, Île d'Oléron **183**
campsite locator **8–9**
campsites at a glance **10–12**
campsites in France **178–183**
Camus More, Portree, Isle of Skye **202–205**
Celtic Camping, St Davids, Pembrokeshire **154–155**
Cerenety Eco Camping, Bude, Cornwall **42–45**
Cleadale Campsite, Isle of Eigg **198–199**
Cliff House, Saxmundham, Suffolk **94–95**
Cnip Grazing, Isle of Lewis **216–217**
Coastal Cabins, Hartland, Devon **229**
Conwy
  Mountain Lodge, Abergele, Conwy **234**
  Trwyn Yr Wylfa, Penmaenmawr **130–131**
Cornwall
  Beacon Cottage Farm, St Agnes **34–37**
  Cerenety Eco Camping, Bude **42–45**
  Cotna Eco Retreat, Gorran **229**
  East Crinnis Farm, Par **40–41**
  Elm Farm, Redruth, Cornwall **32–33**
  Free Range Escapes, St Kew **229**
  Mousehole Camping, Penzance, Cornwall **28–29**
  Teneriffe Farm, Helston, Cornwall **30–31**
  Treveague Farm, Saint Austell **38–39**
  Wild Camping Cornwall, Penzance **24–27**
Cotna Eco Retreat, Gorran, Cornwall **229**
Crows Nest, Filey, North Yorkshire **103–104**
Cumbria
  Ravenglass Campsite, Ravenglass **122–125**
  Woodman's Huts, Haverthwaite **233**

D

Deepdale Backpackers, Burnham Deepdale, Norfolk **100–101**
Devon
  Beryl's Campsite, Kingsbridge **60–63**
  Caffynes Farm, Lynton **56–57**
  Coastal Cabins, Hartland **229**
  Fairlinch Camping, Braunton **46–47**
  Karrageen, Kingsbridge **58–59**
  Little Meadow, Ilfracombe **52–55**
  Ocean Pitch, Croyde **48–51**
  Owl Valley, Bideford **229**
Domaine La Yole, Herault **182**
Dorset
  Eweleaze Farm, Weymouth **70–73**
  Hook Farm, Lyme Regis **68–69**
  Knaveswell Farm, Isle of Purbeck **230**
Dunes at Whitesands, St Davids, Pembrokeshire **156–157**
Dunnet Bay, Thurso, Caithness **226–227**

E

East Crinnis Farm, Par, Cornwall **40–41**
East Lothian
  Harvest Moon, Dunbar, East Lothian **237**
Eigg, Isle of
  Cleadale Campsite, Isle of Eigg **198–199**
Elm Farm, Redruth, Cornwall **32–33**
Elmley Nature Reserve, Isle of Sheppy, Kent **230**
Essex
  The Shepherd's Hide, Brightlingsea **230**
Eweleaze Farm, Weymouth, Dorset **70–73**

F

Fairlinch Camping, Braunton, Devon **46–47**
Frankshore Cabins, Tenby, Pembrokeshire **237**
Free Range Escapes, St Kew, Cornwall **229**
French Riviera
  Les Eucalyptus **183**

G

Gironde
  Camping de l'Océan, Gironde **180**
  Panorama du Pyla, Gironde **182**
Glamorgan
  Heritage Coast Campsite, Cowbridge **176–177**
glamping alternatives **228–237**
Graig Wen, Dolgellau, Gwynedd **140–143**
Grange Farm, Grange Chine, Isle of Wight **82–85**
Grove, Cromer, Norfolk **233**
Gupton Farm, Freshwater West, Pembrokeshire **168–171**
Gwynedd
  Aberafon, Caernafon **132–133**
  Bach Wen Farm, Clynnog-fawr **234**
  Cae Du Farm, Tywyn **144–147**
  Graig Wen, Dolgellau **140–143**
  Llwyndu Farm Hut, Llanaber **234**
  Mynydd Mawr, Pwlheli **134–135**
  Nant-y-Bîg, Pwlheli **136–139**
  Smugglers Cove Boatyard, Aberdyfi **148–151**

H

Hampshire
  Lepe Beach Campsite, Southampton **78–81**
  Muddycreek Farm, Milford on Sea **74–77**
Harris, Isle of
  Lickisto Blackhouse **212–215**
Harvest Moon, Dunbar, East Lothian **237**
Hemscott Hill Farm, Morpeth, Northumberland **118–119**
Herault **182**
  Domaine La Yole **182**
Heritage Coast Campsite, Cowbridge, Vale of Glamorgan **176–177**
Hill Fort Tipis, Dyfed, Pembrokeshire **152–153**
Hillend, Llangennith, Swansea **172–173**

Hook Farm, Lyme Regis,
   Dorset 68–69
Hooks House Farm,
   Robin Hood's Bay,
   North Yorkshire 106–109
Huttopia Côte Sauvage,
   Île de Ré 181

I

Île d'Oléron
   Camping Les Chênes
   Verts 183
Île de Ré
   Huttopia Côte Sauvage 181
Invercaimbe, Arisaig,
   Inverness-shire 200–201
Isle of Wight
   Grange Farm, Grange
   Chine 82–85
   Vintage Vacations, Ryde 230
   Whitecliff Bay, Bembridge
   86–89

K

Karrageen, Kingsbridge,
   Devon 58–59
Kent
   Elmley Nature Reserve,
   Isle of Sheppy 230
Knaveswell Farm,
   Isle of Purbeck, Dorset 230

L

Le Balcon De la Baie,
   Normandy 183
Lepe Beach Campsite,
   Southampton,
   Hampshire 78–81
Les Eucalyptus, French
   Riviera 183
Lewis, Isle of
   Cnip Grazing 216–217
Lickisto Blackhouse,
   Isle of Harris 212–215
Little Meadow, Ilfracombe,
   Devon 52–55
Little Otchan Hut, Halsham,
   East Yorkshire 233
Llwyndu Farm Hut, Llanaber,
   Gwynedd 234
Lochranza, Isle of Arran
   184–187

M

Manor Farm, Cromer, Norfolk
   96–97
Mountain Lodge, Abergele,
   Conwy 234

Mousehole Camping, Penzance,
   Cornwall 28–29
Muasdale, Tarbert, Argyll
   188–191
Muddycreek Farm, Milford on
   Sea, Hampshire 74–77
Mull, Isle of
   Sheiling Holidays,
   Craignure 237
Mynydd Mawr, Pwlheli,
   Gwynedd 134–135

N

Nant-y-Bîg, Pwlheli,
   Gwynedd 136–139
Norfolk
   Amber's Bell Tents, Holt 233
   Deepdale Backpackers,
   Burnham Deepdale
   100–101
   Manor Farm, Cromer 96–97
   Scaldbeck Cottage,
   Holt 98–99
   The Grove, Cromer 233
Normandy
   Camping Bel Sito,
   Normandy 180
   Le Balcon De la Baie,
   Normandy 183
Northumberland
   Hemscott Hill Farm,
   Morpeth 118–119
   Walkmill Campsite,
   Warkworth 120–121

O

Ocean Pitch, Croyde,
   Devon 48–51
Owl Valley, Bideford, Devon
   229

P

Panorama du Pyla, Gironde 182
Pembrokeshire
   Celtic Camping, St Davids
   154–155
   Dunes at Whitesands,
   St Davids 156–157
   Frankshore Cabins, Tenby,
   Pembrokeshire 237
   Gupton Farm, Freshwater
   West 168–171
   Hill Fort Tipis, Dyfed
   152–153
   Porthclais Farm, St Davids
   158–161
   Stackpole Under the Stars,
   Stackpole 234
   Shortlands Farm,

Haverfordwest 162–163
   Walton West Campsite,
   Little Haven 164–167
Port Bàn, Tarbert, Argyll
   192–193

Porthclais Farm, St Davids,
   Pembrokeshire 158–61

R

Ravenglass Campsite,
   Ravenglass, Cumbria
   122–125
Ross-shire
   Badrallach, Dundonnell,
   Ross-shire 210–211
Runach Arainn, Lagg,
   Isle of Arran 237
Runswick Bay Camping, nr
   Whitby, North Yorkshire
   110–113

S

Sands, Gairloch,
   Wester Ross 206–209
Sango Sands, Durness,
   Sutherland 222–225
Scaldbeck Cottage, Holt,
   Norfolk 98–99
Scilly Isles
   Bryher Campsite,
   Bryher 20–23
   Troytown Farm,
   St Agnes 16–19
Scourie, Sutherland 218–221
Serenity Camping, Whitby,
   North Yorkshire 114–117
Shear Barn Holidays, Hastings,
   East Sussex 90–93
Sheiling Holidays, Craignure, Isle
   of Mull 237
Shepherd's Hide, Brightlingsea,
   Essex 230
Shortlands Farm, Haverfordwest,
   Pembrokeshire 162–163
Skye, Isle of
   Camus More, Portree,
   Isle of Skye 202–205
Skysea Camping Park, Port
   Eynon, Swansea 174–175
Smugglers Cove Boatyard,
   Aberdyfi, Gwynedd
   148–151
Stackpole Under the Stars,
   Stackpole,
   Pembrokeshire 234
Suffolk
   Cliff House,
   Saxmundham 94–95
Sussex, East

Shear Barn Holidays,
   Hastings 90–93
Sutherland
   Sango Sands,
   Durness 222–25
   Scourie, Sutherland
   218–221
Swansea
   Hillend, Llangennith
   172–173
   Skysea Camping Park,
   Port Eynon 174–175

T

Teneriffe Farm, Helston,
   Cornwall 30–31
Treveague Farm, Saint Austell,
   Cornwall 38–39
Troytown Farm, St Agnes, Isles
   of Scilly 16–19
Trwyn Yr Wylfa, Penmaenmawr,
   Conwy 130–131

V

Vintage Vacations, Ryde, Isle of
   Wight 230

W

Walkmill Campsite, Warkworth,
   Northumberland 120–121
Walton West Campsite, Little
   Haven, Pembrokeshire
   164–167
Wester Ross
   Sands, Gairloch,
   Wester Ross 206–209
Whitecliff Bay, Bembridge,
   Isle of Wight 86–89
Wild Camping Cornwall,
   Penzance 24–27
Wold Farm, Bridlington, East
   Yorkshire 102
Woodman's Huts, Haverthwaite,
   Cumbria 233

Y

Yorkshire, East
   Little Otchan Hut, Halsham
   233
   Wold Farm, Bridlington 102
Yorkshire, North
   Crows Nest, Filey 103–104
   Hooks House Farm, Robin
   Hood's Bay 106–109
   Runswick Bay Camping, nr
   Whitby 110–113
   Serenity Camping, Whitby
   114–117

Acknowledgements

Cool Camping: Coast

Series Concept & Series Editor: Jonathan Knight

Editor & Project Manager: James Warner Smith

Co-editor: Martin Dunford

Editorial Assistants: Andrew Day, David Jones

Researched, Written & Photographed by:
David Bowern, Anna Chapman, Dan Davies,
Sophie Dawson, Andrew Day, Keith Didcock,
David & Jane Hart, David Jones, Scott Manson,
Andrea Oates, Sam Pow, Paul Sullivan, Hayley
Spurway, Clover Stroud, Dave Swindells, Alexandra
Tilley Loughrey, Ally Thompson, James Warner
Smith, Dixie Wills, Amy Woodland, Richard
Waters, Harriet Yeomans

Designers: Kenny Grant, Diana Jarvis

Proofreader: Leanne Bryan

Indexer: Helen Snaith

Published by: Punk Publishing, 81 Rivington
Street, London EC2A 3AY

UK Sales: Compass IPS Limited, Great West
House, Great West Road, Brentford TW8 9DF;
020 8326 5696; sales@compass-ips.co.uk

Punk Publishing takes its environmental
responsibilities seriously. This book has been
printed on paper made from renewable sources
and we continue to work with our printers to
reduce our overall environmental impact.

We hope you've enjoyed reading *Cool Camping:
Coast* and that it's inspired you to visit some of
the places featured. The campsites in this guide
represent just a small selection of the many sites
recommended online at **coolcamping.com**.
Visit the website to find more campsites and to
leave your own reviews, search availability and
book camping and glamping accommodation
across the UK and Europe.